Families in Context

Emerging Trends in Family Support and Early Intervention

Edited by
Barry Carpenter

David Fulton Publishers
London

David Fulton Publishers Ltd
Ormond House, 26–27 Boswell Street, London WC1N 3JD

First published in Great Britain by David Fulton Publishers 1997

Note: The right of Barry Carpenter to be identified as the editor of this work has been asserted by him in accordance with the Copyright, Designs and Patents Act 1988.

British Library Cataloguing in Publication Data
A catalogue record for this book is available from the British Library

ISBN 1–85346–489–9

Typeset by FSH Print and Production, London
Printed in Great Britain by BPC Books and Journals, Exeter

Contents

Part III: Cultural Perspectives

Part IV: Initiatives in Research and Practice

Foreword

Philippa Russell

> The Family is the fundamental group in society and the natural environment for the growth and well-being of all its members and particularly its children. As such, the family should be afforded the necessary protection and assistance so that it can fully assume its responsibilities within the community. Working with rather than on parents and carers in the interests of children is essential to a healthy society.
>
> (United Nations (UN) Convention on the Rights of the Child)

The past decade has seen an unparalleled interest in (and accompanying debate around) the role, rights and responsibilities of families. The debate has in part been positive. Most governments are moving away from 'crisis intervention' towards refocusing around family support and early intervention. But at the same time there is growing uncertainty within a contract culture about what style of early intervention can actually help children and families and at the same time represent value for money. Equally, there has been an emerging intolerance towards difficult and disruptive children, about parental responsibilities as well as rights, and an increasingly punitive attitude towards those children who do not fit easily within the current framework of services.

In the UK (as in many other countries), the UN Convention on the Rights of the Child has stimulated new interest in children's rights and family policy. It also provides a framework for early identification and intervention, in particular identifying key themes which need to run through any policy developments. These four themes are:

- **participation:** the concept of the child as an emergent and active citizen;
- **provision:** to be made on the basis of a child's right to health, education and care;

- **protection:** acknowledging the right of all children to be safe and protected from abuse;
- **community:** the right to a family life, friendships and inclusion in the local community.

What does the UN Convention mean for families of children with disabilities and special educational needs (SEN) as we move towards the millennium? Firstly, we need to put 'rights' in perspective and acknowledge the changing nature of family life. The past decade has seen major migrations of population, with many communities now reflecting multicultural lifestyles and languages. We are seeing a continuing growth of children living within one-parent families, and a corresponding increase in 'reconstituted' families, with all the complexity of new relationships which these bring. Most countries are seeing major competition between resources for children's services and the needs of an increasingly large and frail elderly population. In consequence, communities and the politicians who allocate resources find themselves facing uncomfortable decisions about the allocation of increasingly scarce resources and definitions of 'need'. The Audit Commission (1994) and others have emphasised the importance of more targeted investment in vulnerable children and families and the need to see prevention as being a critical issue in promoting the 'well-being' of children.

Developing a policy of family support: what do parents want?

> Family support is about the creation and enhancement of locally based or accessible activities, services and networks, with and for families in need. The use of such services will lead to positive outcomes such as alleviation of stress, increased self-esteem, enhanced parental and family competence and behaviour and increase the parents' capacity to nurture and protect their children. Family support operates at different levels... it presupposes integration of services rather than polarisation between crisis intervention and general support in the community.
>
> (Hearn 1996)

Barbara Hearn's model of family support reflects a shift away from crisis intervention towards a longer term approach to family support, which moves beyond the delivery of services towards enhancing the competence and confidence of families to work with their children and feel successful. In terms of early intervention, many families start from a low base and are faced with multiple pressures in becoming the new-style proactive partners envisaged by all three statutory services. Beresford (1995), in a major study of the lives of parents of children with disabilities, emphasises both the importance of listening to the families' 'expert opinions' and recognising the multiple practical difficulties experienced by many families. She notes the 'double jeopardy' of some of the most vulnerable families (e.g. single parents and families from minority ethnic groups) who may need the greatest level of support, but may receive the least. Any intervention programmes targeted at a particular behaviour or perceived 'need' may be ineffective without creating the resources within the family to cope with any extra demand.

Developing effective systems of family support will often be the crucial precursor to more active parent partnership and effective early intervention. Hearn (1996) stresses the importance of asking parents what they need and acknowledging that families will need very individual packages of support, ranging from the very informal 'befriending' to what child protection teams in the USA describe as 'family preservation'. Family preservation presupposes clear criteria and local procedures for the early identification and assessment of very vulnerable families to ensure that services are sufficient, appropriate and acceptable. As the Audit Commission noted in 1994, current professional and statutory services are often poorly coordinated and criteria for support (and outcome measures for any intervention) may be very variable.

A major agenda issue for the next century must be the challenge of identifying:

- what we mean by early intervention, and who is the beneficiary, considering parent, child, the effective use of resources by the agency in question and 'value for money';
- conditions for particular styles of early intervention and what criteria should be used in allocating particular services;
- parents' roles and responsibilities in complying with early intervention programmes, and how we engage with the 'hard to reach' parents.

Carpenter (1996a) reiterates the importance of acknowledging the context for partnership between parents and schools and, in particular, for acknowledging the different lifestyles of families and for building flexibility, sensitivity and communication into any intervention programme. Carpenter also stresses the need to see the family in its broadest context and to recognise the roles (and the needs) of siblings, grandparents and the extended family networks. Most importantly he notes the role of fathers and the importance of developing interventions which engage, encourage and move families forward. Dale (1996), looking at the translation of partnership into practice, similarly stresses the importance of a whole-family approach. She notes that 'theorising' about families must take account of changing family dynamics and wider attitudes towards disability or disadvantage within the community. The family in society is not static. It is multidimensional, and needs will change over time; a message widely echoed by contributors to this book.

The life-cycle approach to family support and family policy poses a number of dilemmas. Currently we have little evidence of the long-term outcomes of different styles of family support (as opposed to outcomes for educational interventions). The Mental Health Foundation (1997), in a report of a committee's inquiry into children with learning disabilities and challenging behaviours, highlights the urgent need to prioritise evaluation and research into the different models currently available and notes the importance of such an approach at a time when evidence-based treatments or interventions are the preferred options for many purchasers. But, as noted below, outcome measures may be different when measured against the family's increased self-confidence, the child's improved behaviour or educational development, or society's satisfaction that a 'problem' has been solved.

The problem-solving approach for society, as opposed to the family or child, is an emerging issue in a number of countries. In the UK, it is reflected in an increasingly punitive attitude towards difficult and disruptive children, with increases in exclusions and preoccupation with youth crime, but few ideas about what intervention to adopt. Notwithstanding the media demonising of certain children and families, there are encouraging indicators that government departments, as well as local services, are moving towards an integrated approach to earlier identification, intervention and ongoing support for families with a variety of special needs. A Home Office White Paper (1997), *Preventing Children Offending,* notes that:

> The Government believes that it is essential to intervene with children at risk of becoming offenders as early as possible. It is also essential to develop strategies for intervention on the basis of sound knowledge of what works.

The document reviews a range of positive initiatives, such as High/Scope (Schweinhart and Weikhart 1993, Sylva 1996), which have been developed outside the criminal justice system, but with a view to supporting the overall well-being of children and families and concludes that: 'On that basis [of evidence on early intervention such as High/Scope], Early Intervention to prevent children offending makes sound financial sense'.

While few readers of this book will be primarily concerned with prevention of youth crime, the message about 'sound financial sense' at a time of major retrenchment in human services makes sense. In effect, we need to evaluate, to reflect and to learn from the different options for early intervention – and we need to look at important issues of sustainability and ongoing support. The family is, after all, for life, yet there have been few longitudinal studies of the lives of families with children with disabilities or SEN. At the very least, we can ask the families.

Early identification and intervention: challenges and opportunities

The concept of early intervention for young children with disabilities and special needs, as developed in the 1960s, has had a profound ongoing impact upon professional attitudes to parents as partners in the early care, education and development of their children. Programmes like Portage (Cameron 1986a) clearly demonstrate that families can be the most effective and economical system for fostering and sustaining the development of a young child.

But we also need to acknowledge a growing debate about:

- the criteria to be used in determining which programme or intervention is likely to be most effective for individual families;
- the outcome measures for successful interventions, with clarity as to whether programmes are directed at long-term cognitive developments for children, greater parental confidence and competence, or for specific issues such as child protection;
- the context for successful interventions, acknowledging that different services may have differing objectives, but that family support will be critical for the development of active partnership;
- the roles and responsibilities of professionals, with greater integration of services to avoid duplication and overlap: some families collect professionals like children collect stamps; others

may receive minimal support, with later difficulties and risk of family breakdown;

- the delivery of services within a changing society, with more working and single parents and with evidence of low take-up of current provision by some families;
- the sustainability and long-term outcomes of early intervention programmes.

Addressing these issues will be challenging. We have the legal framework to do so. But, as Sheila Wolfendale commented (1995), there is a paradox inasmuch as the policy framework does not always live up to its legal context:

> The paradox lies in the fact that parental involvement in assessment and intervention has come so far as to be codified within a legislative framework and yet in being thus codified, the parent–professional relationship is now exposed.

In addressing this paradox, we will need to explore new and innovative approaches to recording, evaluating and developing responses to different styles of early intervention and family support. As the UN Convention on the Rights of the Child tells us, the family is the fundamental group in society and the natural environment for the growth and well-being of all its members. But important questions remain about the most effective and acceptable models of early identification and intervention and how we move away from the concept of 'parents as problems' to a more proactive partnership approach which acknowledges strengths, weaknesses and aspirations within a constantly changing society. This book takes us one step nearer to identifying the answers to these challenging questions.

Acknowledgements

The technical editorship of this book has been skilfully undertaken by Jo Egerton, to whom I am deeply indebted.

I am grateful to colleagues in the Centre for the Study of Special Education at Westminster College, Oxford, who have given constant encouragement throughout this venture. Also to David Fulton and his team who have such a tremendous capacity to offer so many authors the opportunity to be heard.

Finally I, and my co-contributors, are in awe of the families who have shared their stories with us. They are the central focus and core inspiration of this book, and their unique insights will enhance the professional work of us all. At times these families work through emotional pain and personal trauma to share their invaluable stories. We must treasure these gifts, their stories, for they remind us all of our humanity.

Barry Carpenter
Oxford, April 1997

Dedication

To Eleanor Jane, who makes our family complete

Contributors

Anne Bray is director of the Donald Beasley Institute in Dunedin, New Zealand. She is involved in research and education in the field of intellectual disability. For the past eight years, she has led a team of researchers working on a series of research projects investigating issues pertinent to family members of people who have disabilities. She intends to retain this family focus and has another programme of family research planned for the next three years. A grandmother herself, Anne Bray is aware of the limited amount of research in the area of grandparents who have grandchildren with disabilities. The work she has done in this area is an attempt to address this imbalance.

Barry Carpenter is director of the Centre for the Study of Special Education, Westminster College, Oxford; he was formerly an inspector of schools and a headteacher. He publishes widely on a variety of special needs issues. He co-edited (with Rob Ashdown and Keith Bovair) *Enabling Access: Effective Teaching and Learning for Pupils with Learning Difficulties,* which was awarded the 1996 Academic Special Needs Book Award (National Association of Special Educational Needs/Educational Publishers Council). He has lectured nationally and internationally, conducting lecture tours in Australia, New Zealand and Europe. His current research focuses on early intervention and family support. Barry is the father of a child with learning difficulties.

Matthew Carpenter is 16 years old and a student at Henry Box School, Witney, Oxfordshire. He hopes to go to university to study economics.

Katie Carpenter is 12 years old and has an integrated school placement at Wood Green School, Witney, Oxfordshire. She excels in food technology and enjoys reading and writing.

Grace Carpenter is in nursery (kindergarten) education and longs to be in big school! She enjoys ballet and music.

Sue Carpenter teaches at Clanfield Primary School, Oxfordshire, and was until recently co-SEN co-ordinator at Queen's Dyke Primary School, Oxfordshire. She was formerly a deputy headteacher, and is an experienced early childhood educator. She combines her paid employment with that of 'domestic engineer' – managing the Carpenter household.

Maureen Corby is coordinator for the one-year full-time diploma in early intervention in the Centre for Special Education at the Auckland College of Education in New Zealand. Her knowledge and interest in typical child development arose through her teaching career in New Zealand and London. Her knowledge and interest in child development was expanded to include atypical development with the birth of her daughter, who has disabilities.

Tricia David is professor of early childhood education at Canterbury Christ Church College. Tricia has been a nursery and infant teacher, and a headteacher in nursery and primary schools, and a researcher and lecturer at Warwick University. She is known for her many publications, especially *Under-Five – Under-Educated* (Open University Press).

Fernando Almeida Diniz was formerly reader in special needs in education at the University of Greenwich, London. He is now responsible for graduate-level studies, research and consultancy in areas of counselling and guidance, SEN and community education at Moray House, University of Edinburgh. He is chair of the European Association of Teacher Education for Special Needs, and visiting professor at universities in Germany, Portugal, Spain and New York. He is currently undertaking research on ethnic minorities and special education.

Barbara Doyle is a lecturer in the Centre for the Study of Special Education, Westminster College, Oxford. She has worked in the field of special education for 20 years in special schools and in support services for young children in the mainstream sector. While studying for her MA, she researched multiprofessional approaches in early intervention and has a long-standing commitment to collaborative and trans-disciplinary practices in working with families with a child with special needs.

Airi Hautamäki is adjunct professor of educational psychology at the University of Helsinki in Finland. She is a full academician of the International Academy of Pedagogical and Social Sciences of Russia. She has lectured internationally, and publishes widely in her research field.

Elaine Herbert has worked in home settings alongside families and their pre-school children with possible SEN for more than ten years. She retired as deputy headteacher of Solihull's Pre-School and Home Teaching Service in 1996. Prior to this, she worked extensively in the field of SEN in a variety of schools in Birmingham, Liverpool and Solihull and within the Grants Educational Support Training (GEST)-funded parent–partnerships scheme. She is currently engaged in research looking closely at the reactions of fathers to the births of children with special needs. She is married with two teenage sons.

Elizabeth Jones is presently a research student in the school of education, University of Wales, Cardiff, studying early intervention services for children with SEN. She has presented papers at a number of conferences at national and international levels.

Donald Meyer is the director of the US Department of Education-funded Sibling Support Project at the Children's Hospital and Medical Center in Seattle. He conducts workshops for parent and professional audiences throughout the USA and Canada on sibling issues, and how to start Sibshops and other programmes for brothers and sisters of children with special needs. Don was a founder of the pioneering Supporting Extended Family Members programme at the University of Washington. He has co-written (with Patricia Vadasy) *Living with a Brother or Sister with Special Needs: A Book for Sibs* (1996), and he edited *Uncommon Fathers: Reflections on Raising a Child with Special Needs* (1995). He is currently editing *Like It Is,* a collection of 46 essays by young brothers and sisters, which will be published in 1997. Don is married to a special education pre-school teacher and is the father of four children.

Brigit Mirfin-Veitch is a researcher with the Donald Beasley Institute. She is currently involved in research pertaining to family members of people who have intellectual disabilities, and families in which one or more of the parents has an intellectual disability. She has a particular interest in relationships within families where one or more members have an intellectual disability.

Jenny Moir has, for the past ten years, worked as a nursery teacher in a nursery which includes and supports children with learning difficulties and their families. Previously she helped to set up a local education authority (LEA) service to assess the needs of children with possible SEN, working with them at home, in partnership with their families. She has also run a pre-school playgroup.

Philippa Russell is director of the Council for Disabled Children in London (UK). The council supports the National Parent Partnership Scheme Network. She is an honorary member of the College of Child Health (BPA) and a member of the National Disability Council. A parent of a son with disabilities, she has worked with the Department for Education and Employment (DfEE) and the Department of Health (DoH) on the development of guidance on disability and SEN, and works closely with a wide range of voluntary and parent organisations.

Beverley Stewart is a registered psychologist and teacher with postgraduate specialist qualifications in school psychology, special education and family counselling. She is currently employed as area adviser (early intervention) with responsibility for implementing, managing and evaluating early intervention service provision within education in a large multicultural metropolitan area. She has been involved in the development, editing and implementation of national training programmes including 'Towards Inclusion' (1989) and 'Early Start' (1993), both of which promoted the rights of students with disabilities as well as providing a family focus and practical programming for teachers in either the compulsory school or early childhood education sectors. She has been involved on a long-term basis with parent support groups in terms of support, skills development provision and policy contributions on an invited and negotiated basis.

Dee Twiss is a registered psychologist and educational psychologist. She is national service coordinator, and also Auckland area adviser, with the early intervention Special Education Service. She has been closely involved in writing early intervention policy and national evaluation and protocols. She has presented papers at many conferences on early intervention, the most recent of which being the International Association for the Scientific Study of Intellectual Disability world conference in 1996. She has co-written *Parent Pack* (1988) and *Access* (1993) for parents of children with special developmental needs, and has contributed to *New Zealand's Exceptional Children* (eds N. Singh and D. Mitchell). She has had a long-term involvement with parent advocacy groups. She is the mother of a daughter with profound hearing loss.

Pat Vadasy is currently a research associate at Washington Research Institute in Seattle. She co-wrote (with Donald Meyer) *Living with a Brother or Sister with Special Needs: A Book for Sibs*. She has frequently written about families of children with special needs and has a special interest in grandparent issues. Currently she is working, together with Donald Meyer, on a book for grandparents of children with special needs.

Jean Ware is now at the School of Education, University of Wales, Cardiff. She previously taught children with SEN before moving to the Institute of Education, London, where she ran a diploma course for teachers of pupils with severe learning difficulties. She has published books and papers on education provision for children with severe and profound learning difficulties, including *Special Care Provision* (with P. Evans 1987), *Educating Children with Profound and Multiple Learning Difficulties* (ed. 1994) and *Creating Responsive Environments for Children with PMLD* (1995).

Abbreviations

ACAC	Awdurdod Cwricwlwm ac Asesu Cymru
CRE	Commission for Racial Equality
DES	Department of Education and Science
DfE	Department for Education
DfEE	Department for Education and Employment
DHSS	Department of Health and Social Security
DoH	Department of Health
EU	European Union
FCDSs	Nordic families with a child with Down syndrome (2–17 years old)
FCWDs	Nordic families of children without disabilities (2–17 years old)
GEST	Grants Educational Support Training
GP	general practitioner
IDP	individual development plans
IDT	interdisciplinary team
IEP	individualised education programme
IFSP	individualised family service programme
IHC	Society for the Intellectually Handicapped
KS	Key Stage
LEA	local education authority
MCDSs	Nordic mothers of children with Down syndrome
MCWDs	Nordic mothers of children without disabilities
MDT	multidisciplinary team
MOE	Ministry of Education
MSI	multisensorily impaired
NCs	Nordic countries
OECD	Organisation for Economic Cooperation and Development
OFSTED	Office for Standards in Education

PRESAM pre-school assessment model
RNIB   Royal National Institute for the Blind
SCAA   Schools Curriculum and Assessment Authority
Scope   Scope for People with Cerebral Palsy (formerly the Spastics
        Society)
SEN   special educational needs
SES   socio-economic status
TDT   transdisciplinary team
UK   United Kingdom
UN   United Nations
UNESCO United Nations Educational, Scientific and Cultural
        Organization
US(A)   United States (of America)

Part I: Introduction

Chapter 1

Our family

Katie Carpenter, Grace Carpenter and Matthew Carpenter

How many people live in your house?
How many people live in your house?
One, my mother,
Two, my father,
Three, my brother,
Four, my sister.
There's one more. Who can it be?
Ah yes, I know. It must be me.

(children's song)

My family

Mummy:

Mummy's name   is   Sue.   She   is   a   mummy   and

a   teacher.

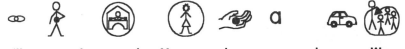

At   home   I   help   Mummy   with   the

cooking.   We   make   cakes   and   biscuits.   Mummy   helps   me

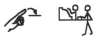

with   my   homework.   Mummy   has   a   red   car.   We

go   shopping.

I   love   my   mummy.

Daddy:

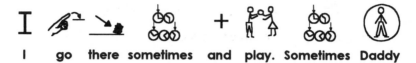

Daddy's name is Barry. He goes to work at college.

I go there sometimes and play. Sometimes Daddy

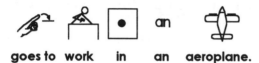

goes to work in an aeroplane.

I like to help Daddy in the garden.

We sing together.

I love my daddy.

Matthew:

Matthew   is   my   big   brother.   He   makes   me   laugh -

he   makes funny faces. Sometimes   we   fight!

He   goes to Henry   Box   School.   He   has

a   motorbike.   I   like   to   sit   on   it.

I   love   Matthew.

Grace:

Grace   is   my   little   sister. When   she   was   a   baby,

I   gave   her   dinner.   We   call   her   Grace   Little!

Grace   and   I   play   weddings.   I   read

stories   to   Grace.   We   do   writing   in   our   books.

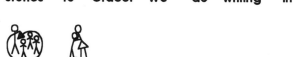

We   cuddle.

I   love   Grace.

Katie by Grace:

Katie is my sister. She plays weddings with me.

She reads books with me. I think she is a

good reader. She gets washed and dressed by herself.

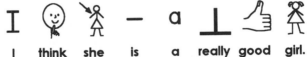

I think she is a really good girl.

She is very special because she wears hearing aids.

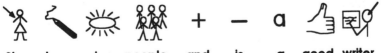

She draws nice people, and is a good writer.

I love Katie because she is a

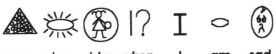

very nice sister when I am sad.

My sister Katie

Katie has been my sister for 12 of the 16 years of my life. I have seen her progress from a podgy little baby to a slender girl. Even though she has Down syndrome, I have never seen her as different to any of my friends' sisters. She is that friendly face that I love and loathe, and I wouldn't change any of her.

I was four years old when Katie entered my life. I was at the age where Katie's difference did not bother me, and the only thing that was different about her was her little nose which made her double cute.

As the years went by, I treated Katie like a sister who was four years younger than me. We played games together, and we had fun together. But then I got older, and though the physical age difference was the same, the mental one became so much bigger. This did not change my perception of Katie in any way; I just took on the role of the older brother.

Katie has had, and still has, what people see as 'strange habits', like reciting dance routines or playing with imaginary people; all normal things that Katie does – to me – but to others they seem a little silly. This irritates me, because silly little girls laugh at her, and silly little boys call her funny names. Katie is so very trusting she does not know what they are saying. She just giggles along with them, blissfully unaware of what they are saying to her. However, they don't say anything like this while I am around! No one picks on my little sister!

She is not 'retarded', 'ill', 'dumb' or whatever other name people wish to classify her under. She has Down syndrome: this makes her different, but nothing more. If those people who try to classify Katie could be more accepting and trusting like Katie then the world would be a better place.

The most prominent thing I remember about Katie is her giggle. She can have fits of hysterics at the drop of a hat. Over the years, I have found it is easier to deal with Katie when she is happy than when she's annoyed. So by various acts of clowning around, I can get Kate to do anything, and turn her tears into laughter or a smile.

One other thing that is at the forefront of my mind when the name 'Katie' is mentioned is her stubbornness. On some days she will want something, and when she can't have it she gets upset. Her temper makes her non-compliant, forcing her to miss out on things that she would enjoy.

The Katie I know now is very different to the one of old. She is more thoughtful, more able to stand up for herself, and a very worthy opponent! She draws unique pictures in her own original style. She is less trusting (not a bad thing), but still a giggler. Stubborn as ever, but developing into her own person. I often wonder what the future will hold for Katie. Will she have a home of her own? A boyfriend? A job? Whatever happens, she will know that she has a brother who will always protect, support and love her.

Chapter 2

Working with families

Sue Carpenter and Barry Carpenter

Beginnings

For a ten-year period, in both Essex and Warwickshire (UK) we worked together developing early intervention groups for very young children with SEN and their families. For us, this coincided with the start of our own period of parenting. This was a unifying factor which led to deep bonds being established with many of our families which still exist today, despite the changes in our professional lives.

The majority of referrals to these groups were received from various professionals (social workers, health visitors, pre-school teachers, paediatricians). We found ourselves working with some very disoriented parents, dismayed at the events life had bestowed upon them. Making their referrals, the professionals used a variety of descriptors of the parents – 'They're very quiet', 'You'll find them very angry', 'They're oozing with aggression.' Indeed, we did encounter parents displaying this full range of emotions, for as Beckman and Beckman-Boyes point out: 'The news that a child has, or is at risk from, a developmental disability, is often among the most frightening and confusing pieces of information that parents will ever receive.' (Beckman and Beckman-Boyes 1993, p. 1). However, what we encountered without fail from all of our families was their love for their child. This is a crucial ingredient for any successful parenting, and one which, as evidence-based practitioners, we are reticent to articulate. It is this natural love that will drive the parents of these children on through the inevitable challenges that will arise as part of the child-rearing process of a child with an SEN. From a mother's perspective, Preethi Manuel (1996) says, 'What is often not recognized is that mums and dads and brothers and sisters have love for the child. They don't necessarily want to abandon that child because it is *their* child.'

In Donald Meyer's collection of essays by fathers of children with disabilities, one father writes:

> Peering into the crib of a child with a disability in the pre-dawn moonlight can bring tears of truly unconditional love – love that will not be based on report card performance, scores as a star quarter-back, or excellent performance as a respected trial lawyer. This love is for who this person *is,* for their qualities, their trials, and for the inner strength they must develop to take their place. It is their struggle – we can only hope and help, watch and love.
>
> (Meyer 1995, p. 25)

Very soon we noticed that both commitment and advocacy emerged from these families, a factor noted by Anne Bray and her colleagues in their New Zealand study (1995).

Acceptance and adjustment

Many parents arrived with us for our weekly meetings in a grief state. Those of you who have experienced deep grief know what a disorientating process this can be: the world goes at one pace, and you are in the slow track; people are talking at speed, you are having difficulty in articulating even one word; tiredness seems unending, and those around you are bursting with energy. How can parents be expected to absorb and understand complex and emotionally charged information? How can they be expected to make sense of the endless round of appointments that are suddenly becoming part of the daily life cycle?

We watched as they emerged from their grief, often into that state commonly known as 'chronic sorrow'. This is a concept that has been highlighted several times in previous decades (Gabba 1994, Wikler 1984). Airi Hautamäki, in her chapter in this book, explores this in relation to the cross-Nordic study on mothers of children with disabilities. Some parents went forward again from this state, but others remained within it. For some parents, the loss of the normalcy of their child would never go away. Deeply caring and excellent parents as they were, there was a sorrow about them that tinged all of their interactions with their child. It was not that they could not feel the joy as their child achieved, or appreciate their child's endeavour, but for them this was the unexpected child, to whom they could never totally adjust. S/he had not been part of their life plan, and the significance of this child's arrival had probably meant a painful adjustment, in either their personal goals or their dreams and aspirations for their family.

An added dimension came for us with the arrival of our daughter, Katie, who has Down syndrome. The subsequent birth also of our daughter, Eleanor, who sadly died of the rare disability, Sacralagenesis, meant that our communion with the parents with whom we were working was very deep. Like them, there were some emotions that seared through us which were beyond words.

Chronic vulnerability

But among the parents in the early intervention group, the knowing look, the empathetic listening helped us all to support and sustain each other through the next round of clinic and hospital appointments. We, along with the parents in our group, identified that we had one factor in common – chronic vulnerability. When your child has a disability/SEN, you do not know what is coming next. 'The arrival of a new baby has a massive effect on any family, but there is a qualitative difference when the baby has a disability or special needs' (Dale 1996, p. 33).

What may appear to be a routine check-up with a paediatrician can be the breaking of another piece of traumatic news. We well remember the mother who, already knowing that her child had a developmental disability, went for a routine blood test only to be told by a paediatrician, in the corridor, that he had a diagnosis of Angelmann's syndrome for her child. Her partner was not present, no family member there to support her: just her and her baby in a hospital corridor.

For ourselves, we have known the devastation of our vulnerability, and the amusement. On one paediatric hospital appointment with Katie, we were told that her heart condition needed further exploration, and we were to see a cardiac paediatrician. This came as a shock. We had thought all was well with her heart.

On the visit to the cardiac paediatrician, he had asked if he could scan Katie's heart. This would involve her lying on a bed, while he passed a monitor over her heart. To prepare Katie for this, we talked to her about the visits she had made to the hospital when her mother was pregnant to 'see the baby in Mummy's tummy', and how she would be able to see her heart on the television screen, just as she had seen the baby. Katie was not keen to lie on the bed, so one of us lay down and held Katie. The gel applied by the paediatrician went everywhere! Katie began to sob, and in her distress looked at us and said, 'But I don't want to have a baby!!' In our opinion, chronic vulnerability is a constant state; it is part of being the parent of a child with special needs.

Changing patterns

We noticed over the years a change in the pattern of babies joining our groups. New causes of disability were emerging. We twice worked with children who were severely brain-damaged due to the heroin addiction of their mothers. This trend has been observed in the USA, where Ball (1996) reported on a national survey that indicated that 375,000 newborn babies a year had been exposed in the womb to cocaine, heroin, marijuana, methadone, amphetamines and pentachlorophenol (PCP). The doctors in this study explained that exposure in the womb to cocaine alone could cause severe damage, including pre-natal strokes, lasting brain damage, seizures after birth, premature birth, retarded fetal growth, breathing lapses, absence of part of the gut and structural abnormalities in genital and urinary organs. The same study noted another sad societal trend: that alcohol abuse in pregnancy was considered to be an even greater problem than illegal drugs. Low birth weight was another factor leading to the identification of SEN. Hallahan *et al.* (1996) report a study from Cleveland, Ohio, which indicated that 50 per cent of extremely low birth weight children have IQs that are borderline normal or lower; 21 per cent of these have severe intellectual impairment. This trend has been similarly observed in the UK (Carpenter 1995a).

Another changing pattern in the ten-year cycle which we observed then, and which has come even more to the fore in recent years, is that we were not only working with parents but with the wider family group: siblings, grandparents and other family members. For many, their families also comprised non-blood relatives. Neighbours and friends were of paramount importance to these families (Carpenter 1996a). Roll (1991) reports that: 'The stereotype notion of the family – two married parents of the opposite sex with two children, who rely on only the father's income – is a reality for only one family in seven today.'

Hence the structure of families is changing rapidly, and now incorporates a range of significant people who take a genuine and shared interest in each other's lives and who will advocate for each other (Carpenter 1996b).

Self-defining families

Recently, we pursued this notion further through a series of semi-structured interviews with 20 families of children with severe learning difficulties. (The children were in the age range of 5 to 16 years.) We asked a simple question about who supported their family. The following list emerged:

- neighbours;
- friends;
- work colleagues;
- church members;
- teachers/school staff;
- link families;
- volunteers from charitable organisations.

We then looked at the main types of support offered by these 'significant others'. Each of the support functions listed below was reported by five or more families in the sample:

- baby-sitting/child-minding;
- transport;
- respite care;
- social activities;
- meals out for the child and/or the family;
- practical help in the home (household chores, maintenance tasks);
- empathetic listening.

In a recent American study by Marianne Ardito *et al.* (1994), they also found that among the 132 mothers of disabled children they interviewed, 58 per cent identified friends as being significantly helpful, with church members (38 per cent) also proving helpful. An interesting factor in this study was that 56.8 per cent of the mothers interviewed were lone parents. There is a real challenge for professionals as to how they cope with the self-defining family. Can they sustain practices which are inclusive to all family members as defined by the family itself? Often our professional forms are not designed to elicit information from non-traditional family members, but if we wish to gain information from all quality sources, then we will need to reflect upon our professional practices and how we adapt to reflect family need. The ecology of the family is first and foremost in their domain, and while subsequent chapters in this book will demonstrate how siblings, grandparents, mothers and fathers are still very influential and important in families, there are also other family members that need to be considered.

Sad and happy

Over the ten years that we worked with families, our diary notes of the sessions demonstrated that the families' perceptions of the services they received from professionals fell into two categories: those which made them happy, and those which made them sad. The type of service delivery that made them sad was traditional and inflexible, expected families to conform to a particular mould, and failed to address the everyday life cycle or the needs that arose out of daily living and gaps in family support there, e.g. baby-sitting, shopping and friendship circles.

A key area of consternation for families was access. Access to services means that families press the button when they have the need. Services need to be relevant to the families themselves, not a set menu prepared by professionals who think that this is what the families ought to have. Professionals need also to be aware of the changing dynamics in the family. What is fine this year, may not be next. A sibling who offers support within a family this year, may next year be at university. The grandparent who was invaluable for baby-sitting may, due to infirmity, not be able to offer this next year. The new baby in the family may bring additional problems, resulting in behavioural disturbance from the child with special needs.

On the 'happy' side of things, there were a range of models of service delivery that were considered to be successful. Home-based approaches were particularly valued. This is a natural environment for the family; it is the ecologically appropriate context. It is the environment in which the family can maximise the input of the services they receive from professionals. Assessment which takes place within the home is naturally going to be the most effective.

The issue of assessment could easily fall into either camp. Many families had had very traumatic experiences of assessment, but some reported positive experiences. They appreciated their opinions were valued and that professionals were trying to work in partnership. A mother recently speaking at a national conference said:

> The professionalism on which you stand is not a different road to the one on which we tread.... It's also a road which is cushioned and softened by the laughter and the smiles of love and the tears of our children. That road is the same road, and when we relate to each other, we have the partnership that dreams are made of. From the educational psychologist who sits with you and tries to translate the

vision you have for your child in the way that his/her report is
written, to the occupational therapist who will make a separate
attachment to your child's wheelchair so the cat can curl up next to
your child, to the midwife who finds a lovely position you can feed
your child in, even though it's completely against her textbook
knowledge.... These are the professionals who are working in the
spirit of the term 'partnership'.

(Manuel 1996)

This quotation reflects assessment that truly addresses family need,
not the professional agenda. Assessment that is about empowering and
enabling the family to progress, to remain together, to find solutions
and not blocks. This is the assessment that families value. Assessment
that heaps indignity on the family cannot be tolerated.

Practical services were particularly valued by families. These
services are not just about professionals talking at families, but offering
something that is interactive for the family or members of that family.
For example, drama groups, play schemes or holiday clubs that include
all children in the family, swimming sessions for the whole family,
family evenings such as discos which again every child and adult in a
family can participate in, fun days for the whole family, where
grandparents, aunts, uncles, friends, neighbours can be invited to come
and join in to celebrate what it is to be a family.

Unique families

Families particularly appreciated the positive approach of many
professionals. The hallmark of practice of these professionals was that
they had treated the family with respect and dignity and acknowledged
the uniqueness of that family. They had not viewed the family as
carrying a terrific burden, but rather as a family that would be self-
sustaining, but at times, like all of us, could need some support. These
professionals enabled the families to be positive and not to become a
'disabled family'. They had been inclusive towards all family members
(e.g. fathers, grandparents), and had not focused solely on the mother
or the child in a deficit-type model.

Finally families demonstrated they appreciated the 'you' factor. They
appreciated services that considered 'you', the individual, the unique
member of the family unit, and had not focused just on the child with
the disability. These professionals had valued the contribution of all

family members (e.g. had allowed the sibling to contribute to the review meetings, had listened to various family members and had not dismissed their contribution because of their age or because they were not blood relatives).

It became clear to us over the years that networking between families themselves was a powerful structure for mutual support. Fundamentally, within the group, we began to see our role as empowering each other in order to empower our children. And what of the children at the heart of these families? What drives families to advocate for quality education, for inclusion in society, for better services? Is it love? Is it fear? Is it that constant nagging worry, 'Who will look after him/her when I'm gone?' It can be any of these, so let us end this section with some words from Michael Williams, a non-verbal disabled person, who summarises the feelings of many parents of children with special needs:

What is the price of a dream not dreamed?
What is the price of a word not spoken?
What is the price of a voice not heard?
What is the price of a vision not imagined?
What is the price of a life not lived?

(Williams 1995)

Part II: Defining family roles

Chapter 3

Finding the family: early intervention and the families of children with special educational needs

Barry Carpenter

Robert and Louise eagerly anticipated the arrival of their first child, and when Clare was born they were elated. Their joy lasted for only a few short moments. Clare's physical disability was obvious – only one ear, her chin depressed into her neck. The paediatrician advised an emergency tracheotomy.

Numbed with shock, Robert and Louise agreed to the operation. During the operation, Clare lost consciousness for 15 minutes. In spite of this she survived. As feeding was clearly going to be a problem, a nasogastric tube was fitted.

During the next week, Clare began to gain weight. Louise noticed that Clare's tongue was exceptionally small. The paediatrician confirmed this and told her that the implication was that Clare would never feed properly. No one counselled Robert and Louise at all during this week. Doctors engaged them in conversations around medical issues; nurses were kind in their ministrations to Clare, and talked to Robert and Louise, but only on care matters.

When Clare was three weeks old Louise noticed that the baby startled whenever she approached her and that Clare did not visually track her face even when she was very close to her. Louise reported this to the nurses, and tests were carried out. She was told (without her husband present) that Clare had a significant visual impairment. Louise asked where she could get help and advice about her child. The doctors shook their heads; they did not know.

Both extended families visited Robert, Louise and Clare frequently. From an initial poor prognosis, it became evident during Clare's first month of life that she was beginning to thrive. Robert and Louise were desperate to talk to someone about Clare and to discover what they could do constructively to aid her development.

Robert's sister happened to know of someone working in special education. Perhaps he could help. Indeed he could; he had a friend working in a regional service for multisensorily impaired (MSI) children. He contacted this friend. Within a day the head of the MSI service had visited Clare and her parents in the hospital. She has kept in regular contact and has taken the parents to visit a Family Centre specialising in the care and support of children and their families with MSI.

After three months in hospital, Clare was finally allowed home for a one-day visit. Prior to this no professional had visited the home; no one accompanied the parents on this occasion. Within two hours of being at home, the portable machine the parents had been given to keep Clare's air passages clear failed to work. The family made an emergency dash back to the hospital.

This story is true. It is the sort of saga one would have expected to hear before early intervention programmes became standard practice from the late 1960s onwards. If only it were; this story happened in this decade in the second largest city in the UK. To this day, those parents have not been given any counselling to help them to come to terms with the shock, grief and despair they have endured in these last few months. The words of Wyman (1986) ring out from this situation: 'Our child is still a child, a child with special needs for whom no miracle cures can be awaited: just herself, just himself, with potential to be explored, love to be given or awakened and a dignity and life to be safeguarded.'

The services this family received, outside the hospital environment, have come via a friend of a friend. Have we not progressed beyond this hand-to-mouth existence? In this chapter, I will endeavour to answer this and other emerging questions.

Where are we now?

Following the growth of early intervention programmes for very young children with SEN and their families in the 1960s and 1970s there came a reflective period during which the efficacy of early intervention was questioned (Marfo and Kysela 1985). Buckley (1994) challenged some of the narrow interpretation of effectiveness. She sought to encourage a more holistic analysis of the benefits of intervention programmes for the whole family, not just in terms of direct quantifiable learning gains for the child with SEN.

In the UK, it would be difficult to assert that early intervention is currently seen as a priority. So many other pressures seem to be reformulating the agenda for all of the major service providers that early intervention at times appears to be lost in the morass. While it used to be a key feature of special education, early intervention has found itself reshaped, redefined and recontextualized through a variety of social as well as educational factors.

Early intervention service delivery in the field of education, where it has retained a high profile, has also been subjected to revisions and even updates. Researchers such as Michael Guralnick (1991) have pointed out that services in the past tended to focus upon helping the child to progress, particularly in areas of motor, language and cognitive development, and that perhaps more attention should be given to the quality of relationships being established between the child and family members. Families themselves have begun to assert this (Fitton 1994, Hebden 1985, Johnson and Crowder 1994). Buckley (1994) has reinforced Guralnick's points and has stressed the danger that the emphasis placed on teaching skills in many early intervention programmes could actually have an adverse effect on parent–child relationships unless they are handled with care and sensitivity. The demands of therapy might have a disruptive effect on families, preventing them from having undirected quality time to spend playing with their children and limiting their contact with friends.

We must give attention to the context in which we deliver early intervention programmes. While the home may be a suitable setting, it is at times isolating. Conversely, the large group situation may prevent us from giving the specific attention that some very young children with SEN and their carers require. Although Portage has its critics, it has certainly made a major contribution in formulating thinking about home-based learning programmes, particularly with its focus upon involving the parents' knowledge about their child. Such programmes have often laid the foundations for the much talked of 'partnership with parents'. Similarly other schemes have been reported which work with families in settings outside their home (Carpenter and Carpenter 1989).

Russell (1994) has drawn our attention to the fact that the successful delivery of home teaching programmes, as a strategy for meeting individual needs in very young children, must acknowledge the interdependence of children's educational, social, care and health needs, and the importance of offering services which reflect the children's and families' culture, lifestyle and other family commitments. The various changes in legislation in the UK have impacted upon how services can provide for very young children with SEN and their families. In every sector concerned with the empowerment of these children – health, education and social services – the changes in legislation have underlined the need for strong interdisciplinary approaches to meet the diversity of SEN that exist in our child population.

We are being faced with children with increasingly complex learning disabilities. These children challenge special educators to devise new and innovative methods of teaching, as well as demanding of professionals in other services new strategies for sustaining and upholding families. More than ever we need dynamic early intervention services that can enable families to work in an active dialogue with professionals towards meeting the needs of their children.

For many years, a variety of professionals have encouraged families in the acceptance of their child with SEN, and the fact that some parents have been slow or reluctant to do this has been attributed to a bereavement response in those parents. At times their irrational behaviour has been likened to grief. While one may endorse many of the similarities that there are between grief and parenting a child with SEN, the reality is that the sadness of having a child with disabilities is constantly renewed, regardless of the pleasures gained from each hard-grafted development. The reality for the family of a child with SEN is that they face recurrent and unpredictable challenges. Not only do they require appropriate early intervention, but they require access to ongoing support at points when they need to push the button.

The families of children with SEN do not seek sympathy, do not want to be patronised. They do want to be valued and treated as equals. They are not interested in being converted to particular educational ideologies or medical or therapeutic doctrines. They desire recognition of the individuality of their child and the uniqueness of their families (Mittler 1996). If we are to meet these expectations in families, and deliver services to very young children with SEN, then we need to achieve a coordinated and coherent approach. What indicators do we know of that would enable us to structure our services in such a way that they can achieve some of the expectations of families and some of the rights of children?

Early intervention: principles for good practice

Recently I have undertaken an international comparative study of three early intervention programmes in New Zealand, Australia and the UK. Through observation and analysis of these programmes certain key principles emerged. The observation schedules used were those designed for the inspection of schools process in the UK (OFSTED 1995). However, the unifying factor which provided the context for practice in all cases was that, within an interdisciplinary team, there was a recognition of the parent as an implicit and fundamental member of that team. The following features were the markers of good practice within this context:

- **Family-focused service delivery** Parents were integral to the whole operation. Not only were they the recipients of services but also were seen as service deliverers themselves. There was a recognition of their unique and invaluable contribution. Siblings were also included in family-based activities. The context for service delivery was balanced between the home, as the environment where parent and child were most comfortable and confident, and community-based settings, such as playgroups or early intervention centres.
- **Parents and professionals mutually valued** This was apparent in the levels of respect and dignity each afforded the other. While the focus of the programme was the child, the context of the programme was the home and other key environments in which the child functioned. The key agents for implementing the programme in a sustained and meaningful fashion were the family. As such, there was a transdisciplinary approach which endeavoured to achieve a seamless and unbroken circle of support for the child.
- **Shared agenda: shared goals** An open and frank exchange of information existed between parents and professionals. Sensitivity to needs and skills was evident, with parental choice embodied as a feature of programme development. The quality of interaction between parent and child was seen to be of paramount importance. There was an acceptance that this at times might take priority over specified goals for development. The approach is well-summarised in the words of Roy McConkey (1994) who said: 'It's farewell to authoritarian experts prescribing similar treatments to "patients", and a welcome to professionals who meet people as people, striving to share their community and valuing the worth and dignity of each as they seek to overcome the adversities of life.'

- **Collaborative working** Programme implementation was a joint venture which recognised the capabilities and limitations of all concerned. Jargon-free communication and flexibility of programme delivery were positive features of the parent–professional relationship. Programmes were enskilling for all concerned – child, parent and professional – acknowledging that we can all learn so much from each other. We never know it all.
- **Effective evaluation** While the programme review meeting had its place, evaluation in these programmes was an ongoing feature. Adjustment to programme goals, contexts and resources were made where the shared feeling was that this was in the child's best interests. Implementation was a shared responsibility and no longer the onerous task of parents who had been dumped with a programme so intensive that it was disorientating to the life of the family. In these programmes there was no place for the precious professional domain; only for skilful, resourceful contributions that would benefit the child and empower the family.

Clearly, in these principles, the quality of partnership between parents and professionals is explicit. In reviewing research in the field of early intervention, McConkey (1994) stated that while there was at present a greater emphasis on families and their role in early intervention, the implications of this new emphasis might not have been worked through adequately in professional practice. He challenged researchers and practitioners to develop and adapt early intervention strategies for use in family homes as well as in clinics and schools, and criticised the continued dominance of research literature by laboratory-style investigation. He also mentioned the need for the focus of professional training to shift from the treatment of individuals to working with families in the provision of teaching and therapy.

Pugh (1994) summarised the aspirations of many authors in expressing the need for a 'developmentally appropriate' curriculum which would provide a quality curriculum for very young children. She further emphasised that 'quality is a dynamic rather than a static concept' (p. 111).

In countries such as New Zealand, early intervention training is offered to teachers on a one-year secondment basis. In the UK there is no such equivalent available, again reflecting the low status of pre-school early intervention-type services. What is very much needed is a transdisciplinary training. Apart from specific training in our respective individual disciplines, when do we ever have the opportunity to study interactively with colleagues from other professions on a long-term accredited basis? Recent evidence has emerged of transdisciplinary training opportunities (Carpenter 1996b, Lacey and Lomas 1993).

McConachie (1994), in reviewing the implications of stress for families with young disabled children, also criticised current professional practice, and argued that the organisational model might owe more to habit than to clear rationale based on the varying needs of the population it serves. The well-supported family might be better equipped to dissipate the stress which has traditionally been associated with the care of a child with a disability (McConachie 1994, Wilton and Renaut 1986). In order to achieve this, however, those professions working in early intervention must reconcile their differences and find a truly transdisciplinary model for service delivery in which they, with parents, are sincere copartners.

Fathers – the peripheral parent?

McConkey has identified fathers of children with disabilities as so-called 'hard-to-reach parents'. Their role as key members in any family needs to be elaborated if we are to appreciate and develop their contribution.

A recent study by Herbert and Carpenter (1994) has focused upon fathers and their role in early intervention. Their study explored the recollections of seven fathers at the time of the birth of their children with Down syndrome. It discussed the disclosures of diagnosis and subsequent contacts the fathers made, both professionally and socially, during the period following their child's birth, both in the hospital and at home. Meyer (1986) suggests that, amid the explosion of research into the role of the father in society as a whole and the family in particular, the fathers of children with special needs were relatively ignored. The literature on the subject is sparse (Hornby 1991, Rodrigue *et al.* 1992). From a review of 24 studies in America, it was found such fathers were rarely consulted and that discussion papers 'allot a page or so to fathers as an aside' (McConachie 1986, p. 43).

The study reported by Herbert and Carpenter (1994) looks at factors such as how the news is broken, parental responses, the content of information and the way in which it is given, professional perceptions of fathers, professional prediction, information-seeking and sources of support. This research aimed to not only analyse the issues identified by the seven fathers, but to retain the emotion of the stories they were telling. Often research, in adopting an analytical stance, divorces itself from emotion. Situations such as the disclosure of a baby's disability is an emotion-ridden experience, and as such we should give credence to the emotions people express and use these to illuminate the situation and improve our knowledge. For example, in this research, professionals had given gloomy forecasts of the effect the child with a disability would have on family life. One general practitioner warned that 'the mother may become mentally unstable and may attempt suicide or harm the baby'; another warned that a marriage might fail. The words of one father illustrated his actual feelings when given such news:

> This must all be a dream – this thought runs through my mind again and again. This cannot happen to us! In this turmoil, I was conscious of the supportive attitude of the hospital staff, that every effort they made was an endeavour to uphold us, to help us to endure the pain and distress that fell upon us as the reality of our baby's disability dawned upon us.
>
> (Herbert and Carpenter 1994, p. 50)

The fathers in this study described situations such as 'the calm after the storm' when, once the family had returned home from the hospital, the fathers received no specific help from the professionals. All help was focused on the mother and the baby. The fathers' needs were not addressed or, perhaps, even noticed. They were seen as the 'supporters' and as such adopted the role society expects – that of being competent in a crisis (Tolston 1977). All seven fathers talked of returning to work and trying to search for normality and keep a sense of reality in their lives. One father explicitly said: 'I returned to work, but in a fog. The feelings of disorientation were enormous and even simple tasks took considerable effort to complete. This only served to disempower me even further' (Herbert and Carpenter 1994, p. 53).

In this study, the extended families were found to be a major source of support to the fathers. It could be conjectured that the existing familiarity at the emotional level with other family members generated a climate of openness in which fathers could reveal their true feelings. In some societies they have a concept of what, in Maori culture, is known as 'whānau'. A whānau is a Maori social structure incorporating all age ranges, interests and experience. It is a form of extended family but does not necessarily comprise blood-relatives (*see* Ballard 1994). Current social trends cry out for the emphasis to be not only on the family but also on the extended family of the type defined above. Families themselves are identifying their supporters, and professionals need to give careful consideration to how they will case-manage these non-traditional family units (Levy *et al.* 1996).

In a further debate about the role of fathers in early intervention, Carpenter and Herbert (1994a) challenged the traditional model of professional support. Fathers became particularly distressed that once they had returned to work many appointments were made with professionals for their wives and children during the time when they were at work. Having constantly to receive anxiety-raising information through their wives was not always a positive factor in the relationship, and caused some fathers to feel that they were, inevitably, the secondary partner.

The key innovations for good practice arising from this study are discussed in greater depth in Chapter 5. They centre around issues of:

- training;
- coordination of services;
- accessibility;
- networking;
- consumer needs;
- the needs within the family.

Fathers, like early intervention itself, can find themselves marginalised, on the periphery of activity, secondary to the key carer who inevitably seems to be the mother.

Conclusion

Can early intervention 'come in from the margins'? Can it re-emerge as a key strategy for supporting families, empowering parents and meeting the highly specific development needs of infants with disabilities?

A reconceptualisation of early intervention is needed if it is to gain credibility with families. Already there are reports of parents rejecting the reliance the early intervention programmes of the 1970s placed on professionals (Brown 1994a) and stressing the need for normality (Wills 1994). Philip Ferguson (a parent) and Adrienne Asch (who is disabled) say that:

> The most important thing that happens when a child is born with disabilities is that a child is born. The most important thing that happens when a couple become parents of a child with disabilities is that the couple become parents.
>
> (Wills 1994, p. 248)

The days of professionals as experts have gone; what are needed now are informed supporters. McConkey (1994) rightly points out that in the previous three decades many early intervention programmes 'floundered in simplistic notions about intervention and a failure to appreciate the difficulty of changing human behaviour patterns' (p. 7). Where these programmes were successful was in the positive approaches they engendered in parents. They gave a basis for meaningful transaction between (often) mother and child.

We must move our focus of support from the dyad of mother and baby alone to the triad – mother, father and baby (Herbert and Carpenter 1994). This is a message to carry forward, but also on which to elaborate. Indeed, mindful of the need to regenerate the extended family ought we to be giving time to other members of this family structure, grandparents in particular? Peter Mittler (1994) has pointed out that since grandparents now live a much longer active life, and since transport and telephone can bring families together across longer distances, then perhaps we should take their potential contribution into account in professional assessments of family resources and influences.

To achieve closer collaboration with parents, professionals must acknowledge the uniqueness of each family. We may be asking professionals to operate in new ways, and as such we have to recognise that there is a training need. Previously many packages attempted to train parents as teachers or therapists (often with limited success) (Basil 1994a, McConachie 1986). Has the time now come for parents to offer training to professionals? If we genuinely have an equal partnership, each valuing the contribution of the other, then there are messages to share about our philosophy and practice. Such information is not necessarily for the conference hall or even seminar room. Rather it is an ongoing training process, encapsulated in the dialogue of support and interaction between parent and professional.

Early intervention *is* coming in from the margins. It is reasserting its role as the first means of support to families of children with disabilities, and it will prove its efficacy based on their evaluation, not on quantitative clinical research data. Through holistic approaches to family support differentiated intervention strategies will emerge that enable the child with a disability to be seen as a contributing family member; there will be an expectation of success for the child and celebration of its achievements.

Such approaches will ensure that no family member is marginalised (i.e. fathers) and that they have a right to direct involvement in the parent–professional dialogue (Carpenter 1995b). This will challenge some professionals and demand a radical reappraisal of the structure of their role and their style of delivery, but, if we want quality early intervention, such a review is fundamental to re-establishing the place of early intervention as a valid and valuable resource to families.

Early intervention is not an optional activity; it is a crucial contribution. The facilitating foundations of early intervention can ensure quality of life for the child with a disability and its family. Do you wonder, as I do, what opportunities have already been missed for Clare? What irrevocable damage has been wreaked on her family? For the sake of present and future generations early intervention *must* come in from the margins.

Chapter 4

Mothers – stress, stressors and strain: outcomes of a cross-Nordic study

Airi Hautamäki

Introduction

The study is a part of the cross-Nordic research project, 'Families of children with disabilities in the Nordic countries: a Nordic research project for analysing the medical and social effects of disability on the child, the family and society'. The research project was initiated by the Nordic School of Public Health in Gothenburg (Köhler 1990), Sweden, which coordinated the project through Evy Kollberg. The participants of the Nordic research project were Evy Kollberg (Sweden), Airi Hautamäki (Finland), Arvid Heiberg and Thomas Öye (Norway), Stefan Hreidarsson (Iceland) and Jan Kirkegård (Denmark). Each was responsible for the data collection in their own country. I want to express my gratitude to the team for the opportunity to collaborate in the fruitful exchange of ideas, and for the opportunity to test my theoretical ideas on the Nordic data.

A cross-sectional Nordic study with a representative sample of non-handicapped children

The cross-sectional study reported here focuses on Nordic families with a child with Down syndrome (FCDSs), emphasising the impact which that child makes on the family's social, psychological and physical well-being and lifestyle as a whole (Kollberg *et al.* 1997). A control group was included from a comparison study, carried out in 1984–5, with a representative sample of families of 2–17-year-old children without disabilities (FCWDs) in the Nordic countries (Köhler 1990). Thus, it is possible to compare both family demographics and lifestyles of 479 FCDSs to those of approximately 10,000 FCWDs in the Nordic countries.

Mothers: the primary care-givers

As mothers are usually the primary care-givers of the children (Chodorow 1990, Hautamäki 1995), they are assumed to be most vulnerable to the presumed stress and the accompanying health risks associated with the sustained care-giving roles inherent in mothering a chronically ill child (Zimmerman 1988, 1992) or a child with a disability.

A study done by Gustavsson (1989) also indicates that the impact of a child with a disability on the mother's allocation of time for different activities is greater than that on the father's. The greater-than-average care-giving responsibility will markedly reduce the mother's alternative options for action (Barnett and Boyce 1995). The mothers' presumed stress and ill health are analysed in the context of family life, particularly in terms of the conflict inherent in mothering: that between care-giving tasks and options for alternative life projects (Gustavsson 1989, Hautamäki 1996).

The conflict inherent in mothering: between care-giving and other life projects

I have modified the functionalist (Ferguson and Ferguson 1987) model proposed by Gustavsson (1989), with the help of theories of mourning (Bowlby 1960, Cullberg 1975, Solnit and Stark 1961) and complemented by the idea of chronic sorrow (Wikler *et al.* 1981), to describe the gradual working through of the novel life situation by the mothers of children with Down syndrome (MCDSs). The model (*see* Figure 4.1) illustrates the developmental sequence in which Swedish mothers adjusted to their child with a disability: first seeking initial solutions to the above-mentioned conflict; gradually rejecting the first ones; then developing their own personal solutions for living with their child (Hautamäki 1996).

Expressed in psychodynamic terms, the discovery of the child's disability was a shock. It shattered the parents' omnipotential expectations of their parenthood: that they would be the ideal parents of the dreamed-of baby (Solnit and Stark 1961). In the 'meeting the new life situation' phase, the reality of the practical consequences of the child's disability, and the resulting conflict between the parents' personal interests and those of the child emerge.

The first solution to the conflict arrived at by the mothers studied by

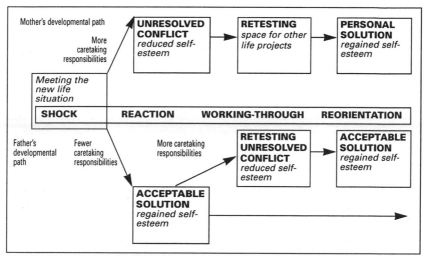

Figure 4.1   Parents' adjustment to and working-through the conflict
between caring responsibilities and other life-projects

Gustavsson (1989) was characterised by abstaining from any other life
projects. The mothers stayed at home, abandoning their earlier plans
and ambitions in order to provide for and look after their child. One
may hypothesise that this first solution – the mother totally devoting
herself and her time to the child – was not only the appropriate reaction
of a sensitive mother to the needs of her disabled infant, but also may
have been an attempt on the part of the mother to heal and to restore
her partly damaged self-image of herself as a mother. It represents the
first reaction to finding a way to cope with and work through the
feelings connected to the demolition of expectancies.

However, the first solution was unworkable; the mothers became
frustrated and exhausted. In other words, they were at their wits' end.
This is the 'unresolved conflict' phase: the culmination of the first
solution which excessively restricted the mothers' options for
maintaining their self-esteem in other areas of activity in their lives.
Moving on from this, they tested solutions to the conflict that would
neither betray their child nor themselves: the 'retesting' phase. Usually
the new solution presupposed that some of the caring responsibilities
would be delegated to the father or to the social services system
(Gustavsson 1989, Hautamäki 1996).

On the basis of the model, it is assumed that if it is not possible for
the mother, as the child grows up, to resolve satisfactorily the conflict
between the care-giving responsibilities and the options for other

activities and gradually, naturally, recover her self-interest, then the unresolved conflict, in the long run, may result in stress. The sorrow and anxiety related to unmet expectations in regard to the course of the mother's own life and that of her child will well up more strongly at crucial points of the family's life-cycle.

The Swedish fathers usually followed quite a different path to the mothers in working through the conflict. Their first solution was characterised by giving total priority to their work and abstaining from any caring responsibilities. They usually became involved only when the mothers retested their first solutions. Gradually they assumed some of the care for their disabled child, and this initiated the difficult conflict between caring responsibilities and other life projects for them, too. In coping with this conflict, they also had to work through the shattering of their expectancies concerning the child and to develop new priorities. Thus the fathers experienced stress later than the mothers, especially if they had difficulties in resolving the conflict between their perceived caring responsibilities and options for other life projects (Gustavsson 1989). (See Hautamäki (1996) for a presentation of the results concerning the Nordic fathers of the present study.)

Method: procedure and instruments

In 1984, a postal questionnaire was distributed to a sample of FCWDs (N = 10,422) representing each of the Nordic countries. In 1991, detailed questionnaires were administered to a sample of FCDSs (N = 479) in these countries in order to obtain comparable data on families with a child with intellectual impairment. Down syndrome was chosen because it can be reliably identified at birth. The mothers responded anonymously to the questionnaire.

The criteria for inclusion in the sample were:
- established diagnosis of Down syndrome in the child;
- age of the child between 2 and 17 years;
- place of residence: both urban and rural families were represented in the sample.

The average return rate exceeded 70 per cent.

Some health indicators were used in the study to measure the assumed outcome of prolonged stress. The mother was the respondent to the questions concerning the number and type of psychosomatic symptoms, e.g. headache, sleeplessness, stomach troubles, back pains, lack of appetite. The age of the child was used as a crude indicator of the family's life-cycle stage.

The effects of a child with Down syndrome on parental well-being, especially the mother's health and the family's lifestyle, were estimated by a two-way analysis of variance. The mother's reported psychosomatic symptoms were estimated using two factors:
- presence of a child with Down syndrome in the family;
- the age of the child with Down syndrome.

Full factorial models were estimated which allowed testing for significant interactions between the effect of a child with Down syndrome and the other factor.

Family demographics of FCDSs

A demographic comparison was made of 479 FCDSs to those of 10,422 FCWDs. The socio-economic status (SES) of FCDSs was higher than that of FCWDs (Hautamäki 1996), especially regarding the mother's and the father's educational level and the family's SES (Table 4.1). Stoneman (1989) stresses that the comparisons of children with Down syndrome with other disability groups often result in groups dissimilar on demographic factors, such as maternal age and SES. This is also the case in the present study, although the comparison group consisted of children without disabilities. It is important to note the differences in the mothers' educational levels because the mother's educational level permeates all the socialisation practices in the home (Gecas 1979), related as it is to the mother's feelings of control over her life and her child's development (Hautamäki 1982). These educational and socio-economic differences between the samples of children with Down syndrome and those without disabilities were due to a slight over-representation of families from urban areas caused by the sampling procedures used for the FCDSs sample.

Studies have suggested that the stress associated with additional caring responsibilities would lead to higher than normal levels of divorce in families with children with intellectual impairments (Gath, in Byrne and Cunningham 1985). In this FCDSs sample, the proportion of single-parent to two-parent families was about the same as in the FCWDs sample (Hautamäki 1996). The presence of a child with Down syndrome did affect the mother's, but not the father's, working hours. Significantly fewer MCDSs had full-time jobs.

Family characteristics	DS	NHC	X²
Mother's education			
Low-level education (completed compulsory education)	52.1	70.3	66.68***
High-level education (completed some further education)	47.9	29.7	
Age			
< 35	27.9	39.8	26.21**
> 35	72.1	60.2	
Employment			
Full-time work	35.8	50.0	35.32***
Part-time work	38.5	31.3	
Housewife	25.7	18.7	
Father's education			
Low-level education (completed compulsory education)	56.8	69.5	29.52***
High-level education (completed some further education)	43.2	30.5	
Employment			
Full-time work	85.7	82.7	4.03
Part-time work	7.4	10.5	
Not working	6.9	6.8	
Family residential area			
Metropolitan area (including suburbs)	48.9	33.7	46.23***
Densely populated area (> 3,000 inhabitants)	23.7	33.8	
Scarcely populated area (< 3,000 inhabitants)	27.4	32.5	
Socio-economic status			
Working class (blue-collar)	27.2	37.9	16.32***
Civil servants (white-collar)	72.8	62.1	
Family finances			
Low-income	46.4	44.9	0.40
High-income	53.6	55.1	
Number of parents in the household			
Two-parent family	90.6	91.8	0.86
Single-parent family	9.4	8.2	
Number of children in the household			
One child	23.4	25.0	9.05*
Two children	40.1	44.8	
Three or more children	36.5	30.1	

Note: *p < 0.01, **p < 0.001, ***p < 0.0001.

Table 4.1 Family demographics of FCDSs (N = 479) and FCWDs (N = 10,600)

Results

The number of psychosomatic symptoms of MCDSs

The number of reported psychosomatic symptoms (once a week or once in two weeks) of MCDSs was greater than for mothers of children without disabilities (MCWDs). Fewer MCDSs were without any psychosomatic symptoms and more of them reportedly suffered from two or more psychosomatic symptoms than MCWDs. The percentage of women who reported no psychosomatic symptoms was related to SES and parenthood. The answer 'No psychosomatic symptoms' was more frequently given by rural than urban MCDSs, by mothers who were well-educated, from two-parent families, were working full-time or had white-collar jobs with high incomes (Hautamäki 1996).

The mother's reported psychosomatic symptoms in relation to the age of the child and in relation to regional differences

One factor that is assumed to mediate the stress experienced by the mother is the age of the child, connected as it is with the parents' life-stage expectations and expectancies in regard to the child's developing competencies. The number of the mother's reported psychosomatic symptoms was explained by the type of family (FCDSs or FCWDs) (F = 18.51, p < .000) and the age of the child (1 = 2–6-year-olds; 2 = 7–12-year-olds; 3 = 13–17-year-olds) (F = 4.37, p < .013). The number of psychosomatic symptoms reported by a MCDS was higher in all age groups and increased more rapidly as the child reached adolescence than for MCWDs (Figure 4.2).

According to the ecological psychological approach (Bronfenbrenner 1979), characteristics of the larger environment have an impact on proximal events within the immediate setting. The different ecological contexts of rural and urban environments may mediate the reaction to the child's disability. The differences between MCDSs' and MCWDs' psychosomatic symptoms were typical for the metropolitan and densely populated areas with the MCDSs suffering more from psychosomatic symptoms than MCWDs. However, the results were not so typical for sparsely populated areas (type of family being the explaining factor, F = 22.20, p < .000, in addition, interaction between the family type and residential area, F = 3.26, p < .039) (Figure 4.3).

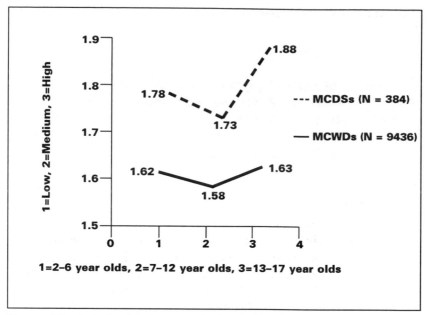

Figure 4.2   Relationship between the level of mothers' reported psychosomatic symptoms (N = 384 (MCDSs) and 9,436 (MCWDs)) and child's age

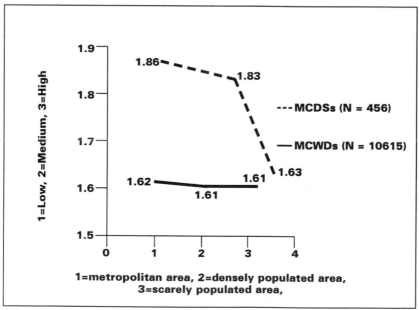

Figure 4.3   Relationship between mothers' reported psychosomatic symptoms and regional differences (N = 456 (MCDSs) and 10,615 (MCWDs))

These results are discussed from different points of view later in the chapter.

Diminishing expectations: the answer to dreams realised in different ways in various ecological contexts?

The results were examined in terms of diminishing maternal expectations as the child grows up (assumed to be the core of the concept of chronic sorrow (Wikler *et al.* 1981)). Raising a child always involves expectations oriented towards the future, e.g. expectations of how to organise life at the next life-stage when the child can manage more on his/her own. The MCDSs' expectations for the futures of their pre-school-aged children were, in general, optimistic. However, their expectations in regard to the future of the school-aged child, and in particular the adolescent child, became more pessimistic. The mothers did not believe that the child could live an independent adult life without the help of outside support systems. According to the analysis of variance, the increasing age of the child (F = 5.93, p < .003) and the residential area (F = 2.87, p < .058) explained the diminution of expectations (Figure 4.4). It may be hypothesised that, as the child grows up, temporary gaps between what the mother expects the child to master on his/her own and the level of the child's self-regulated activity appear. In the context of each developmental task, the mother's culturally defined and established expectations are contrasted with the child's actual capabilities. These periods of diminishing expectations may increase the amount of stress the mother experiences.

In particular, decreasing expectations of the ability of the child with Down syndrome to live an independent life with increasing age were typical of urban mothers. A comparable decrease was not found among rural MCDSs, whose expectations of an independent adult life for their children were generally more optimistic. The rural mothers living in scarcely populated areas also regarded their children's disability as being less serious than the average urban mother and mothers living in densely populated areas, e.g. municipalities. According to the analysis of variance, the residential area was the factor contributing most to the mothers' conception of Down syndrome (F = 6.02, p < .003). In addition, there was an interaction between the residential area and the child's age (F = 2.92, p < .021) (Figure 4.5).

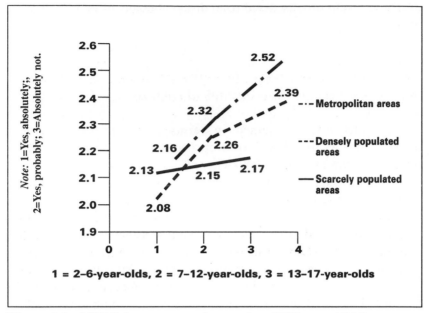

Figure 4.4 MCDSs' responses to the question, 'Will your child live an independent adult life?' (N = 449)

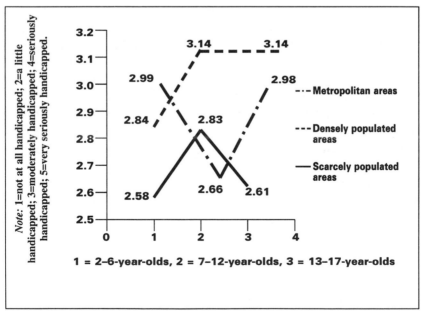

Figure 4.5 MCDSs' perceptions of the seriousness of their child's disability (N = 449)

The mother acting as the external support system of the child's daily activities

Usually the mother is the one who acts as the self-regulating other of the child's daily activities because the child does not develop the self-regulative capacities necessary for autonomous activity. A variable concerning maternal guidance was constructed (a sum of how often the mother plays with her child, goes to the theatre or to the cinema with the child, does homework with the child, reads to the child, or participates in hobbies with the child). The incidence of maternal guidance of children with Down syndrome did not differ from that of other children during the children's pre-school and early school years. However, as the children became adolescent, the need for maternal guidance decreased more rapidly for children without than for children with disabilities. Obviously these children needed their mother for initiating, maintaining and monitoring their activities. The main effects were the child's age (F = 1304.07, p < .000) and the type of family (F = 18.52, p < .000) and interaction between variables (F = 42.63, p < .000) (*see* Figure 4.6).

A sum of the variables was also constructed for the child's

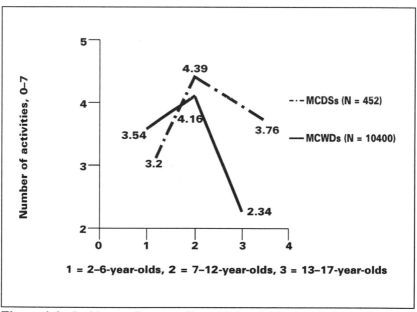

Figure 4.6   Incidence of maternally guided activities in relation to the child's age for MCDSs and MCWDs (N = 452 (MCDSs) and 10,400 (MCWDs))

independent leisure-time activities. The differences between children
without handicaps and those with Down syndrome increased rapidly
from the early school years onward (Hautamäki 1996). Thus, the
MCDS serves as the external support system for the child's leisure-time
activities throughout his/her adolescence to a greater extent than does
the MCWD.

The mothers' restricted leisure

It is hypothesised that the increase in psychosomatic symptoms
reported by mothers of school-aged children is related to the continuing
constriction of opportunities for alternative life-projects in work, in
leisure and in social activities. Lastly, when the child goes to school,
the mother's internal(ised) expectations concerning the child's growing
independence in learning and social activities will probably conflict
with what the child is capable of managing on his/her own. The mother
does not expect herself to be constrained in the same way by a school-
aged child as by a toddler. It is probably the mother's expectations of
an increasing degree of freedom in her life that changes her
interpretations of her life situation and thus the emerging feelings of
restriction may promote stress.

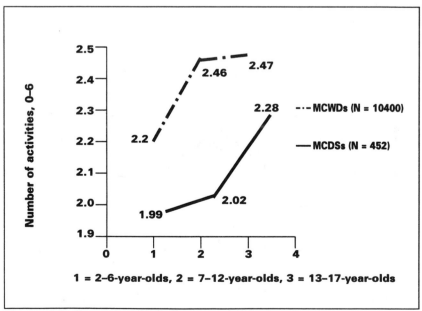

Figure 4.7   Sum of the MCDSs' and MCWDs' leisure-time activities in
relation to the age of the child (N = 452 (MCDSs) and 10,400 (MCWDs))

A sum of the variables consisting of the mother's leisure-time activities (hobbies ranging from cultural pursuits to sports, social activities, participation in educational courses, trade union activities) was constructed. Leisure-time activities of the MCWDs steadily increased during the child's early school years; as s/he became more autonomous, the mother had an opportunity to enlarge the scope of her leisure-time activities. Thus, the differences between the MCDSs' and MCWDs' leisure-time activities were most pronounced among 7–12-year-old children, becoming more equal during the children's adolescence. The main effects were type of family (F = 24.28, p < .000) and the child's age (F = 51.15, p < .000) (Figure 4.7).

The MCWDs' satisfaction with their leisure increased steadily from a higher than average level, when the children were pre-school-aged, to a high level of satisfaction, as the children approached adolescence. The MCDSs stayed at an average level of satisfaction, and their satisfaction differed markedly from the mothers of adolescent children without disabilities. The main effects were the child's age (F = 79.26, p < .000) and the type of family (F = 50.97, p < .000), and interaction (F = 4.26, p < .014) (Figure 4.8). There was a growing dissatisfaction that may be related to the MCDSs' unmet expectations of gradually increasing opportunities for leisure-time activities.

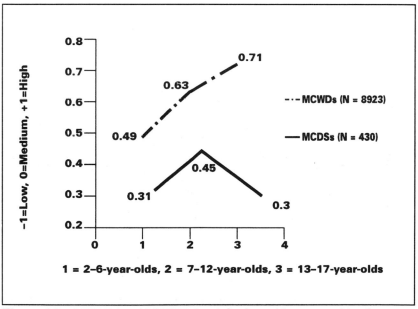

Figure 4.8 MCDSs' and MCWDs' satisfaction with opportunities for leisure time in relation to the age of the child (N = 430 (MCDSs) and 8,923 (MCWDs))

The mothers' satisfaction with their life

The parents of children with Down syndrome also had fewer opportunities to spend leisure time together in activities outside the home, without their children. In FCWDs, the parents' shared activities steadily increased as the child grew up, while the increase was slower in FCDSs. These differences did not decrease even during the child's adolescence (Hautamäki 1996).

On average, the mothers were satisfied with their family situation and their opportunities for joining activities with their husbands: the MCWDs being very satisfied and the MCDSs being relatively satisfied. The level of satisfaction with the family situation differed among MCDSs and MCWDs throughout their life cycles, and the difference between the two groups did not decrease as the children reached adolescence (Hautamäki 1996).

The frequency of the mothers' social contacts with relatives and friends was higher among MCWDs than among MCDSs. The results may be interpreted according to Wehn and Sommerschild (1991) and Byrne and Cunningham (1985), who suggest that the informal social networks of mothers of children with a disability are often smaller, more intense and more closely knit, and whereas they offer support, they may also generate some stress. As some of the children do not develop the social skills necessary for the mastery of equal and symmetrical adolescent peer-group relations, the mother is obliged to integrate the child within her own social activities. The child usually takes part in her social relations, and, consequently, the mother's social contacts may be restricted to those people who accept the child's disability (Hautamäki 1996).

In the present study, the child's personal social contacts and the mother's evaluation of his/her loneliness were investigated. A child with Down syndrome had fewer social contacts than a child without disabilities of the same age, and, additionally, the number of peer interactions decreased during the child's adolescence. The MCDSs thought that their school-aged children were much lonelier than did the mothers of younger children with Down syndrome. Children without disabilities, regardless of their ages, were not regarded as lonely by their mothers (Hautamäki 1996).

The child with Down syndrome develops his/her self-regulatory capacities in his/her social activities, a kind of peer competence, more slowly than does his/her peer without disabilities. Consequently, the child with Down syndrome takes part in his/her mother's social activities to a greater extent than do adolescents in general. The satisfaction with social contacts was moderately high among MCWDs and increased steadily as the children grew up. The satisfaction of MCDSs was, on average, stable but decreased as the child entered adolescence. The MCDSs did not seem completely satisfied with the way their social contacts were organised, depending on the child's age (Hautamäki 1996).

The presence of a child with a disability restricted the mothers' opportunities to work outside the home and, for those who were working, the greater incidence of illnesses of the child with Down syndrome had an impact on the number of hours worked. MCDSs had more absences from work because of the child's illnesses over a three-month period than did MCWDs, the trend decreasing for both groups as the children became older. But the child's frequent illnesses may heighten the mother's multiple role stress (Hautamäki 1996).

The MCWDs were generally satisfied with their work situation, and this satisfaction with their work steadily increased as the child grew up, in contrast to the MCDSs. The MCDSs were less satisfied, and their satisfaction with the work situation actually decreased as the child entered adolescence (Hautamäki 1996).

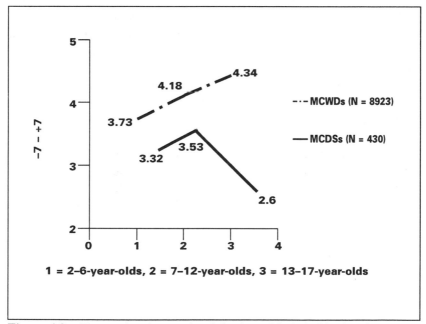

Figure 4.9   The mothers' general satisfaction with their life-situation (N = 430 (MCDSs) and 8,923 (MCWDs))

For both groups of mothers, the satisfaction with their state of health decreased as the years passed and psychosomatic symptoms increased. However, there was a steeper decline in the MCDSs' satisfaction with their state of health over time, and their health actually deteriorated faster than the health of MCWDs (Hautamäki 1997).

If we look at the mother's overall satisfaction with her life-situation, the trends for the two groups of mothers were quite distinct. MCWDs were generally satisfied with their life-situation, and their satisfaction actually increased as the children entered adolescence. The MCDSs were moderately satisfied with their life-situation, but their satisfaction decreased as the children grew up. The main effects were the type of family (F = 62.35, p < .000) and the child's age (F = 58.89, p < .000) and interaction (F = 12.74, p < .000) (Figure 4.9).

The mother's involvement in advocacy

The present study contained a comparison between FCDSs and FCWDs (Köhler 1990) and, consequently, the lifestyle of FCWDs was implicitly used as a kind of positive standard when measuring how families function. The FCDSs were studied in terms of what they seem to lack in accordance with a 'deficit model' of thinking (*see* Bernstein 1975). The FCDSs were not studied in terms of their own lifestyle and the coping mechanisms that are unique and meaningful for their life-situations.

But even in this kind of comparison, some outcomes are found that may be considered positive from a parental empowerment point of view. The MCDSs were more involved in different organisations and had more contact with people who were in a position to influence decisions concerning the child and the family or to influence different societal matters in general decisions that affected children with a disability (Hautamäki 1996).

The greater involvement of the MCDSs in societal matters that affect the child and the family has to do with a position of advocacy evolving among mothers of a child with a disability. As Wright (1976) notes, the parents' reorientation enables them to refocus their attention from themselves to problems concerning their child as s/he is confronted with the demands of the real world. The parents might become mission-oriented. They certainly need this kind of orientation in order to fight for and get the services they need for their child. Thus, the parents gradually begin to channel their energies into helping their child to solve and to overcome problems that are related to his/her unique way and rhythm of learning, as s/he confronts with the culturally defined requirements of new developmental tasks.

Discussion

As this study is cross-sectional, and not longitudinal, the results may also reflect age–cohort differences. There is a time-lag of five years between the sample of FCWDs and the sample of FCDSs. However, the changes during these five years in the historical and social contexts of the two samples are not so great as to invalidate the comparison (Stoneman 1989). With the exception of the mother's age and working hours, the demographic differences between the samples compared reflect differences in sampling procedures rather than real differences between the two populations.

Is it futile, feudal nostalgia, in the wake of the concept of 'Gemeinshaft' (Tönnies 1887), to conclude that there are factors in the families' lifestyles in scarcely populated areas which appear to buffer the strain of mothering? Is the child with a disability more easily integrated into the daily activities of the parents on a farm, and, generally, into the social activities of the neighbourhood? Is the stigma (Goffman 1963) of deviant behaviour less related to Down syndrome? Does the informal social support for the families with a child with a disability function better in rural areas?

Hallden (1992) makes the distinction between two ways of viewing child-rearing: as being or as a project. Do the parents living in rural environments define and experience the meaning of their child's disability in a different way than urban parents do; child-rearing as 'being', rather than as 'project', in agreement with the vital fatalistic view that rural dwellers have towards life? A more fatalistic view of the development of the child, inherent in the 'being' concept of child-rearing, makes a child's disability easier, in a narcissistic sense, to endure because the child's disability is less threatening to the image of good-enough parenthood desired by the parents. But if the child is conceptualised as a developmental 'project', mainly regulated by the goal-directed and deliberate efforts of more highly educated parents, then the child's disability may be interpreted as a greater narcissistic blow to the internal(ised) images of good-enough parenthood (complemented by an idea of good-enough children) sought by the parents, particularly those living in urban areas?

If the child is disabled, it is more difficult to combine successfully some of the omnipotentially tinged requirements of adulthood as defined by our current standards: firstly, by self as an identity project (Giddens 1991). It is living according to a cultural model where the ethos of self-denial, hard work and responsibility for other persons (Björnberg 1992) is largely replaced by an ethos of more unlimited self-fulfilment coupled with sole responsibility for oneself. The idea of self as an identity project implies the continuous commitment of developing oneself through work and education, a process in which individuals creating themselves are even presumed to transcend the ageing process inherent in biological lifespan.

Secondly, there is the project of the child (at best, moulded into the perfect child). The concept of the child as a project implies taking seriously the incessant increase in new demands presumed to be related to the optimal, equated with the maximal, development of a child (Beck-Gernsheim 1992). Both these ideas of modern, industrialised society, child-rearing as a project, and self as an identity project are probably more typical to metropolitan areas. The urban mother of a child with a disability experiences a sharpened, hard-to-solve conflict between, on the one hand, her commitment to her work and education, and, on the other, responding to the constantly growing demands for the development of her child. (For the results concerning the Nordic fathers, see Hautamäki 1996.)

To alleviate maternal strain, it is important to help the mothers solve the conflict between caring responsibilities and other life projects in a way that makes it possible for them to maintain their self-esteem through finding the optimal balance between their needs and the needs of the child. Each mother must develop her own priorities in such a way that she feels that she neither betrays her child nor is overly compelled to deny her own needs. The interventions by various agencies should alleviate the maternal strain by offering services to the family that make it possible for the mother to develop space for other activities in life at the same rate as MCWDs do, as the children develop their age-paced mastery in learning, social activities and work. These services should ideally be tailored to each family to fit the unique cultural features of their way of life and to meet the needs articulated by the family members themselves, as they try to work out their own meaning and ways of coping with the new and challenging situation, the task of growing up together with their child with a disability.

I would like to dedicate this article to the brave, courageous and utterly persistent Nordic mothers in my study, the invisible heroines of everyday life. Many of them would agree with the last lines in Robert Frost's poem, 'The Road Not Taken':

Two roads diverged in a wood, and I –
I took the one less traveled by,
And that has made all the difference.

Chapter 5

Fathers: are we meeting their needs?

Barry Carpenter and Elaine Herbert

Introduction

The ability of early intervention programmes to minimise declines in the development of very young children with disabilities has been identified, through literature and research, as a significant outcome (Guralnick 1991). This position has not been reached without a struggle, which has included a considerable debate about the efficacy of early intervention. Early developments in early intervention programmes laid their emphasis on the professional imparting skills to the parent. Many detailed programmes arose which could be used by professionals aimed at parents; for example, Portage (Shearer and Shearer 1972) and the Carolina Curriculum (Johnson-Martin *et al.* 1990). While Portage has its critics, others would argue that it has been a major platform on which many early intervention programmes have subsequently been developed (Cameron 1986b, Russell 1994).

Buckley (1994) has sought to give a state-of-the-art position on early intervention in the UK, and in so doing has defined early intervention as the 'general term used to describe programmes of educational therapy designed to accelerate the development of children with disabilities in the preschool years' (p. 13). The Finnish researcher, Mäki (1994), identified the primary task for early intervention as facilitating development and decreasing developmental risks for children with learning disabilities.

More recently the move has been towards family-focused models of service delivery. Such approaches acknowledge the child's context, for children do not develop separately from this context but are always in interaction with their environment (Gallimore *et al.* 1989). Buckley and Bird (1995) in their recent guidance to parents on early intervention emphasised that 'the most important gift parents can give their baby is to ensure that he or she is a much loved member of a stable family group' (p. 1). Family-centred intervention is not without its critics: for example, Brinker (1992), who suggested that the focus should be on the processes through which a team works with a family, although he acknowledged that no individual by training, experience or natural personal qualities has a monopoly on wisdom.

This view would not be widely shared, for many researchers and practitioners feel that family-centred models are both more humane and dignifying to the child and its family. This is not to diminish the qualities that an early intervention team should possess. The early intervention team should be a team that includes the family at its centre. As such this team, even at times of uncertainty and anxiety, should be self-supporting and self-sustaining. Indeed families could provide resources to other families to assist in solving problems. Sensitive interaction within the early intervention team will enable the family to change its contribution to that team during the period of the early intervention programme (Simeonsson and Bailey 1990). The dimensions of family involvement may increase or decrease depending on the vulnerability the family may be feeling at a particular time. As with any child-rearing process, it is not always a bundle of fun and non-problematic. But we must acknowledge that families of children with disabilities are first and foremost families, and while our early intervention approaches may be positive in their focus, there should be space for and acceptance of the full range of emotions experienced by any family.

Family-centred approaches to early intervention have been strengthened in the USA through legislation. Public Law 99-457 formally requires an individualised family service programme (IFSP) to be prepared. This is now the subject of much debate regarding family inclusion, parent participation and professional role definition (Bailey *et al.* 1990, Campbell *et al.* 1992). The IFSP is an essential ingredient in family-centred early intervention. Ideally this document is designed by parents and includes areas of emphasis that reflect parent resources, concerns and priorities for themselves and their children. While in the UK there is not the same strength of legislation, there is no reason why this latter practice should not be adopted by early intervention practitioners in any programme record they construct between themselves and families. The IFSP in the USA marks a shift away from the individualised education programme (IEP), which was professionally driven and developed on the basis of a process whereby professionals share with parents evaluation information and desired goals and objectives. This shift is bringing with it a considerable need to present information in 'parent language' as opposed to professional jargon (Campbell *et al.* 1992).

Mattus (1994), alongside Mäki (1994), further stressed that the purpose of family-centred intervention is to empower families, and she recommended an ecological approach to the assessment process in which the involvement of the family is pivotal. This standpoint is entirely compatible with research from Atkins (1994) who suggested that we should view the family as a microculture which displays the key characteristics of any culture. Ecological assessment requires the participation of parents in addition to professionals (Ferguson and Meyer 1991). Its purpose is to gather information about children's real lives: their activities, interactions, experiences and peer contacts in natural environments, both inside and outside the family. Observation is critical to ecological assessment. In moving from child-centred/transactional models of early intervention towards family-centred models, we are challenged by a more complex model of human development which suggests that the boundaries of human development are not only influenced by the characteristics of children, but also are set broadly by the ecology of the child's experiences (Garbarino 1990, Sameroff and Fiese 1990).

Any strategy that we can evolve that empowers families is to be applauded. For it is the family who will bear the main responsibility for the child with disabilities throughout their childhood, their transition into adulthood, and beyond. Families are the sustained influence and the sustainer of the child with disabilities. Professionals, by the very nature of their work, come and go; families do not – they remain. Our task should be to value each family member. Mirfin-Veitch and Bray (this volume) highlight the need to value grandparents, while other authors have identified the needs of siblings and their capacity for support to the child with disability (Meyer and Vadasy this volume, Newson and Davies 1994). The positive advocacy by siblings of a child with SEN has been highlighted in the UK by the interactive work of organisations such as Contact-a-Family (Shelley 1996) and NCH Action for Children (Atkinson and Crawford 1995).

Our research has centred on a family member who has been identified in the past as 'hard-to-reach' (McConkey 1994). This is the father. While not wishing to isolate the role of any family member, and wanting to support and sustain the family as an interactive and holistic unit, it is important to appreciate the dynamics of the role and potential contribution of each family member, particularly if they are to form part of the early intervention team.

Background

The second author of this chapter, Elaine Herbert, has worked as a member of an early intervention team which subscribes to the philosophy articulated in the preceding paragraphs – that of valuing and empowering each family member (Carpenter and Herbert 1994b). It recognises the 'equivalent expertise' of parents (Wolfendale 1989) and subscribes to a consumer approach advocated by Cunningham and Davis (1985). While every verbal or written description of the service will include 'working in the home setting with *parents* of pre-school children with special needs' (Jowett and Baginsky 1991) for 'parents' one should read 'mothers', for it is they who generally have daily care of the pre-school child and work alongside the home visitor. In addition to providing ideas for activities and strategies to be used, all team members are conscious of the non-judgemental support they offer each family (Herbert 1994). As the contact becomes more relaxed, and confidence in each other develops, many mothers recall the events and their feelings at the time of the birth of their child.

It was decided to carry out a small project with nine mothers of children with Down syndrome. The size of this research sample was determined by two criteria: firstly, the demographic focus of the group and the need for the results to be relevant to the development of the service for which the researcher works; secondly, the manageability of the group size within the working caseload of the researcher. As such this was a practitioner-led enquiry carried out in the spirit engendered by Lawrence Stenhouse who argued that practitioner research is vital but also that small-scale studies contribute to the accumulated body of knowledge (Stenhouse 1975). The study concluded that, despite the growing research into the optimum method of disclosure of diagnosis (Cunningham 1994, Hornby 1991, Jupp 1992) and the availability of support services (Lacey and Lomas 1993), there was little coordination between professionals working with families, that the mothers felt isolated, that their needs were rarely met within the community, and particularly that they believed that their reactions had been different from those of their partners. From this analysis and the literature review undertaken alongside it, an increasing awareness developed about how little was known about the reactions of fathers in these circumstances, particularly in the very early days following the birth (Hornby 1991, McConachie 1986, Rodrigue *et al.* 1992).

The original study

The researcher decided to redress the balance and carry out a comparitive study with the fathers of the same children. Mindful of the reactions of the mothers, who had become very distressed when recalling the events and their perceptions of the fathers' reactions, it was decided to make a formal approach to the fathers emphasising the academic focus of the project and the lack of current first-hand information available. (This approach was in direct contrast to the approaches made to the mothers, when an informal verbal request had been made.) It had been anticipated by the researcher that some of the fathers would refuse to participate. However, in the event the seven approached agreed to be interviewed. (Two could not be contacted as they had left the area.) Five stressed that they were happy to cooperate as they 'knew the interviewer', with one adding that he would do so because she was not 'a prying individual interested only in research for its own sake'! As the fathers were not available during the day, the interviews took place during what are considered to be unsocial hours – the evenings. This need to carry out the interviews during these times may in part account for the lack of information available because, as Collins (cited in Meyer 1986) states, in order to gain access to this 'hard to reach' group, researchers might have to work at weekends and in the evenings.

The length of the interviews and the apparent ease with which the fathers spoke surprised and moved the researcher. They appeared keen and eager to talk, and it was concluded that this could be attributed to the fact that they felt that at last someone was listening to them (Cunningham and Davis 1985).

The information gathered

The fathers' recollections of the events surrounding the births seemed particularly clear and mirrored almost exactly those of their partners. They too were critical of the disclosure of diagnosis interviews and felt that they were given too much information about secondary complications, such as heart defects, when they were 'numb', 'angry' and 'in shock'. Comments were made reiterating their wives' feelings of 'lack of coordination' in professional contribution – as one father stated: 'They have guidelines for double glazing salesmen, why not for something like this.'

They perceived themselves as 'different' from other parents of very young children very quickly and were constantly watching others for reactions conveyed verbally or non-verbally (i.e. body language).

Many felt that the choice of words could have created a more positive image of their child, unlike the following words from a consultant: 'I've examined your baby and quite honestly I don't like the look of her; she has all the characteristics of Down's syndrome.'

It has been estimated (McKinley 1994) that each general practitioner (GP) will have one new patient with Down syndrome in a career of over 30 years, but surely the good practice necessary when talking to patients in distress or when giving any form of 'bad news' is no different in situations such as these. Clarkson *et al.* (1996) have recently reported on fathers' comments on health services, reflecting again ambiguities in the system.

Families of the parents were identified as sources of support, and the parents who took part in the study were all fortunate that they were geographically close to their own parents. The fathers acknowledged that in these early days they would also have liked to have spoken to 'someone outside the family' and thought that a third party would have made 'dialogue easier' with their partners. Despite initial optimism, contacts made with other families did not always result in the hoped-for outcomes of friendship and support (Byrne *et al.* 1988).

Six of the seven fathers felt that they needed to be strong and assume the role of protector – being 'competent in a crisis' (Tolston 1977) – and consequently may have suppressed feelings of grief.

At home

The seven fathers in the study were in full-time employment and returned to work very quickly after the mother and baby returned home. They felt this would 'keep some normality in our lives'. One major finding of the study was that ongoing information about the development of the baby was received via their partner who maintained contact with visiting professionals during the day. This, they felt, combined with the lack of accessible and relevant literature, meant that they remained relatively uninformed about their new child. The fathers recognised that despite the fact that they were not 'first time fathers', they did not have a frame of reference in which to place their new baby and felt that they were at 'the bottom of the learning curve' (Kelly 1955).

When the research report was read by the father of a child with a disability (who was not part of the research sample), he found parts of it deeply motivating. Key findings not only reinforced his own experiences and feelings, but also enabled him to reflect and refine his personal experiences. It was decided that further useful exploration of the study area could be achieved if the two parties combined for they both felt that, however thorough researchers are in investigating topics such as these, they can never articulate the depth of emotion experienced by the parents of a child with a disability. They felt that through an analysis such as this they could give a holistic overview of the parent–professional partnership (Carpenter and Herbert 1995a).

Implications for practice

From our original research, six key themes emerged which had implications for professionals desiring to be part of the early intervention team with families. (For a full discussion of these themes, *see* Herbert and Carpenter 1994.)

- training;
- coordination of services;
- accessibility;
- networking;
- the issue of consumer needs;
- consumer model of parental involvement.

The needs within the family

Our interviews with fathers led us to conclude that they perceived themselves to be, at times, the 'peripheral parent' (Carpenter and Herbert 1994a). We must shift our emphasis in the parent–professional dialogue from the dyad of mother and child, to the triad (*see* Figure 5.1).

But beyond this we should include the extended family. Extended families were found to be a major source of support to the fathers. It could be conjectured that the existing familiarity at an emotional level with other family members generated a climate of openness in which fathers could reveal their true feelings. Our father commentator stated:

Is it the child that remains in each of us that causes us to turn to our own parents in times of despair? Certainly, the unquestioning

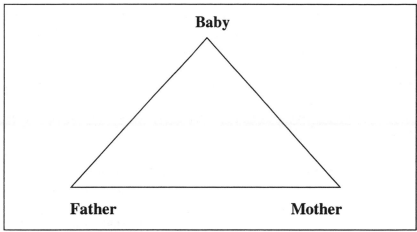

Figure 5.1   Triad of interaction

support of members of our extended family helped greatly with establishing the valued place of our disabled child in our family. Their capacity for support is endless: Is it duty? Is it love? Whatever the reason, the emotional dialogue we have with our extended family has at times been our salvation.

Our definition of the extended family is crucial here, for if we include only blood-relatives then we may be excluding people who have a deep bond with the family, and offer quality support at a variety

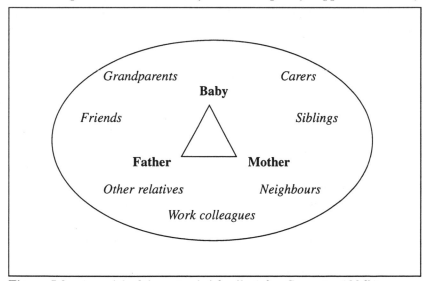

Figure 5.2   A model of the extended family (after Carpenter 1996b)

of levels – social, emotional, psychological or practical. The extended family can be represented diagrammatically (*see* Figure 5.2). Hence we are affirming the contribution of all extended family members, but illuminating from this research the needs perceived by fathers who, unfortunately, at present regard themselves as the secondary partners.

The 'Involving Fathers' (IF) project

Following our initial findings (Herbert and Carpenter 1994), the first author of this present chapter extended the research to look at how schools were involving fathers – the IF project (Carpenter 1995b). The analysis of this questionnaire survey has highlighted issues regarding rhetoric and reality.

The survey

A questionnaire was sent to the headteachers of 20 special schools, each of which was known to have a positive attitude towards parental involvement in the education of their children.

The purpose of the survey was:
- to collect information about the attempts made by these schools to involve fathers (often regarded as the secondary partner in education) and the level of success which these attempts had achieved. It was hoped to draw on the experience and detailed knowledge of the headteachers with regard to their own client group;
- to identify examples of good practice, and in the process allow them to examine critically their own strategies for encouraging fathers to take a more active role in school life.

The IF project has been established to monitor and stimulate parental involvement which actively includes fathers.

Six open-category questions were sent to the schools. The questions themes related to:
- fathers in the life of the school;
- the involvement of fathers in particular events;
- events and groups open to fathers;
- strategies for conveying information to fathers;
- the school event most popular with fathers;
- general observations on involving fathers.

For the purpose of this chapter, the following discussion will focus on the outcomes of Question 6 which gave a global view to the involvement of fathers in the life of the school.

General observations on involving fathers

Schools were asked if they cared to make any further observations on the issue of involving fathers more closely in the life of the school or the education of their children. The most commonly identified observations are listed below. (Comments included in this list were made by three or more schools.) Schools reported:

- existence of role stereotypes;
- they felt that fathers responded to specific task involvement;
- a positive response from fathers;
- particular problems of fathers in relation to children with learning difficulties;
- a desire for suggestions on how to involve fathers;
- a wish to involve more fathers;
- a lack of interest locally in education;
- cultural differences;
- involvement related to the age of the child.

(n = 20)

Role stereotyping dictated the view that the mother was the primary carer, and had the day-to-day management of the child. School was an aspect of the child's life, and therefore the mother's responsibility as part of the mother–child relationship.

Work commitments often contributed to this view; one school confessed that the professional dialogues and documents were often rather mother-oriented. Overall fathers were seen as choosing to adopt a watching brief of a more global nature or were less inclined to be involved, finding it difficult for a wide variety of reasons.

Fathers who were asked to help with a specific task were usually pleased to do so; they preferred a practical involvement rather than discussion. Fathers needed a purpose to be involved, such as fund-raising, mending, building or minibus maintenance. Active interest in school life thus became more confined within a precise area rather than across the board. Issues of direct relevance to their own child attracted fathers more readily, especially questions of residential care and benefits. Although fathers were pleased to become involved when approached directly, headteachers felt that they had to know the father and his skill areas in order to ask. This was a vicious circle – how to know the father in order to ask for help if he never comes into school? This has been an observed trend in other recent studies (Bray *et al.* 1995).

Five schools asked for suggestions from the survey on how to increase the number of fathers involved, and four more agreed that a higher level of involvement would be desirable. But there were particular problems associated with fathers which had a bearing on their reluctance to participate. Fathers, it was felt, often had unrealistic expectations of their child's ability, they took longer to come to terms with or were embarrassed by the child's limitations. Some fathers resisted the move to respite care although the mother, as the primary carer, needed help. One school of 56 children had little contact with 20 fathers and none whatsoever with 16. What was the reason for this? Were they shy, or hadn't they the time? Did they find the school difficult, or could it be they just didn't want to know?

In some areas there was a general lack of interest in schools and not much involvement of either parent. Three schools noted that cultural reasons were a factor, and that with a large ethnic minority group deep-seated cultural and social expectations were involved. Almost all communication with Bengali families is through the father; he is the decision-maker, the translator and the family representative at meetings. Although this would suggest a high rate of involvement, cultural considerations dictate that fathers attend the more formal meetings but not social events. (For a further debate on cultural issues, *see* Diniz, this volume.)

Three schools mentioned that the involvement of fathers was related in some degree to the age of the child. In the early years, fathers were frequently at school, closely involved with their child during an initial period of coming to terms with the learning difficulties. In later years a deeper understanding and acceptance of the child resulted in a reduction in attendance, although fathers remained involved in decision-making through discussion with the mother. Later still, when their child was around 14 to 15 years of age, the fathers' interest was rekindled as their child was preparing for transfer to further education or to work experience. This was an area in which fathers felt they could speak with some experience, as opposed to the subject specialisms of the curriculum.

Practical considerations also played a part where schools had a large catchment area. One school noted that a significant number of their parents had learning difficulties themselves, and that good communication would always present a challenge.

It was encouraging to find that six of the schools reported a positive attitude on the part of their pupils' fathers, many always having had a good level of interest and involvement. More fathers were available than formerly because of localized pockets of unemployment. Fathers who were involved with the school were praised for being keen and enthusiastic, and, when contact was made with others, they proved to be supportive and interested. However, even these schools admitted that the situation could be improved by making more home visits at a time when fathers were available, and by restructuring the school day to hold reviews in the evenings. It was universally felt that when fathers could be enabled or encouraged to attend, their contribution was invaluable.

Concluding comment

We continue to search for strategies which are inclusive towards fathers and which aim to involve them in all facets of the care and education of their child with learning disabilities. Ultimately we believe that the deeper involvement of the father with his child unifies the family, empowers and strengthens that family, and leads them to the shared joy which is a family.

Chapter 6

Meeting the unique concerns of brothers and sisters of children with special needs

Donald Meyer and Patricia Vadasy

Introduction

Throughout their lives, brothers and sisters will share many, if not most, of the concerns experienced by parents of children with special needs. They will also face issues that are uniquely theirs, many of which are documented in the research in clinical literature. Yet many professionals who work with families of children with special needs may not be aware of these concerns, or know how to address them in their work. This chapter will summarise the major findings on siblings' concerns and opportunities as discussed in the research and clinical literature and by siblings themselves. Following this is a summary of strategies to help parents and service providers address sibling concerns and of practices that agencies can adopt to assure that brothers and sisters are a part of their working definition of 'family'.

Concerns experienced by brothers and sisters of people with special needs

Information

A most basic need siblings experience is for information about the disability or illness (Lobato 1990, Powell and Gallagher 1993, Schorr-Ribera 1992). This need for information will change through their lives. As young siblings, they will need information to understand the nature and causes of the disability and to prevent misconceptions that develop when they are left to interpret events on their own. Because pre-schoolers are such concrete thinkers, explanations about disabilities should be very simple and clear. Lobato (1990) observed that children as young as three years are able to detect that a sibling has problems, and therefore that this is not too early an age to begin sharing explanations about a disability (cf. Grace's contribution in Chapter 1).

Once they reach school age, brothers and sisters often need information both to satisfy their own growing curiosity about their brother's or sister's disability as well as to respond to questions posed by their classmates and friends. Throughout their childhood, siblings may come to hold erroneous beliefs about the cause of the disability, sometimes blaming their brother or sister, or even themselves, for causing a brother's or sister's cerebral palsy or cancer. One sister commented:

> My sister's diagnosis is very strongly connected in my mind to nail polish. She was getting into that kind of stuff and I wasn't and so I thought it was kind of gross. I thought she got a rash because of the nail polish, which then caused the cancer.
>
> (Naomi, age 22, in Sourkes 1990, p. 12)

These misconceptions can be prevented when siblings receive the level of information that matches their age and needs.

As brothers and sisters move into their teenage years, many wonder what roles they will play in the lives of siblings in the days to come. Many assume that their futures will be more restricted than those of their peers. At a sibling panel, one 17-year-old sister of a medically fragile child said:

> My sister and I have this picture of the future, this plan. We are going to buy a house together. Neither of us will get married. One of us will work days, the other nights. That way we can care for our brother around the clock.
>
> (Meyer and Vadasy 1994, p. 44)

Another concern expressed by teens regards their own child-bearing potential (Parfit 1975). Often fears about the hereditary nature of the disability are unfounded, but siblings need information and reassurance to that effect. In the event that the condition does have a hereditary basis, older siblings, prior to their child-bearing years, need an opportunity to learn about the genetic implications of the disability (Murphy 1979).

Adult siblings who look after the affairs of their brothers and sisters face challenges similar to those faced by parents of newly diagnosed children. Many find themselves thrust into a world of regulations, acronyms and agencies, struggling to negotiate a maze of social service programmes. They frequently struggle by themselves as few social services proactively provide information to adult brothers and sisters.

Isolation

Brothers and sisters may feel various types of isolation, such as when they are excluded from information available to other family members (Bendor 1990), ignored by service providers (Doherty 1992), or denied access to peers who share their often ambivalent feelings about their siblings (Meyer and Vadasy 1994).

In families where there are only two children, a typically developing child may miss having a brother or sister from whom they can seek advice or with whom to share their thoughts, hopes and dreams. As one brother wrote:

> It was hard. They were telling me stuff that I really didn't understand. At that time he and I were really close. He was getting sick, and we couldn't do much. I was wondering why he couldn't do things any more. And if I got into an argument and hit him, I was always afraid my hit would cause him to die. I felt lonely not having a brother to play with or beat up.
>
> (Murray and Jampolsky 1982, p. 40)

Siblings may feel isolated from their parents and feel they should not bother them with troubles that, from their perspective, are not as important as those of their siblings. In a study of school-age children with cancer and their healthy siblings, Cairns *et al.* (1979) found that siblings showed greater distress than did patients in the areas of perceived social isolation, perception of their parents as overindulgent and overprotective of the sick child, and fear of expressing negative feelings.

Guilt

Young siblings may have feelings of guilt about having caused the disability or being spared the condition. In her study, Koch-Hattem

(1986) found that siblings often blamed themselves for having a role in their brother's or sister's illness. Koch-Hattem also found that siblings experienced survivor's guilt, and spoke of their desire to trade places with their seriously ill brother or sister.

Siblings may also feel guilty about their own good health and abilities (Binkard *et al.* 1987). As one sister wrote:

> I feel bad when John sees me going off with my friends and wonders why he doesn't have many. He'll be at home when I'm out having fun, and it makes my mom feel bad. I feel guilty and don't know how to handle it.
>
> (Sue, age 17, in Binkard *et al.* 1987, p. 13)

All siblings engage in some forms of conflict, like teasing, arguing and name-calling. These sibling conflicts are believed to serve a constructive purpose in that they teach children how to manage and resolve differences and disagreements (Bank and Kahn 1982). However, even these adaptive conflicts are more likely to produce feelings of guilt when one sibling has special needs. Parents who do not understand the value of normal sibling conflict may blame the typically developing child for his/her role in these interactions, and may prevent siblings from expressing their anger and aggression within the family in useful ways.

Older siblings may feel guilty about moving away from home and leaving the burden of care with the parents (Grossman 1972). One sister commented that going away to college was initially a relief: she did not have to care for her brother who has Down syndrome and could sleep in. By mid-college, she felt guilty about not helping, and felt the need to provide her parents with respite (Nester 1989, p. 1).

Another sister wrote:

> When I moved out of my mother's house, I was distraught and overwhelmed by responsibilities. Even the process of moving had to be negotiated on a compromise; I agreed to be near enough to my mother and brother so that I could get to them quickly in the event of problems. This proved to be prophetic, for there were countless days and nights when I was called upon by my mother to help her in a crisis and handle my brother on difficult days.
>
> (Zatlow 1992, p. 13)

Resentment

In many families, brothers and sisters have feelings of resentment because the child with special needs has become the focus of the family's attention, is permitted to engage in behaviour not allowed other family members (Bendor 1990, Podeanu-Czehotsky 1975), or excused from chores expected of other children. One brother told us during a group for teenage siblings:

> My brother gets away with murder! He never has to empty the dishwasher because he has Down syndrome. But he can empty the dishwasher! You know how I know? Because when my parents aren't around, I make him empty the dishwasher!

Bendor (1990) found that some children were frightened by the anger and resentment they experienced and lacked a way to express their feelings. The adults in a sibling's life need to understand the reasons for this resentment in order to help the sibling handle this difficult emotion. Although the one child's needs may make it difficult, parents, say brothers and sisters, should endeavour to set aside time to spend with their other children.

Perceived pressure to achieve

Siblings may experience difficulties in handling parents' expectations for them and the perceived pressure to achieve in academic areas, sports or behaviour (Coleman 1990). One brother noted:

> Ever since I was a child, I have been put into that role – rescuer, perfect child, the one who would make everything right. And all the time while this craziness was going on in my family, I was trying to maintain my grade point average to go on to college and become a doctor.
>
> (David, in Leder 1991, p. 22)

Siblings often experience pressure to compensate for the child with a disability (Murphy 1979, Schild 1976). Although this pressure sometimes comes from parents, Coleman's study (1990) suggests that the pressure frequently comes from siblings themselves.

Care-giving demands

In some families, these increased expectations are expressed in the form of increased care-giving demands, especially for older sisters (Seligman 1979). The early research on siblings of children with disabilities often focused on the care-giving demands of siblings, especially sisters. These early researchers found that sisters tended to be more adversely affected by having a brother or sister with a disability (Farber 1960, Fowle 1973), and oldest daughters were often pushed into a surrogate parent role and given heavy care-giving responsibilities (Cleveland and Miller 1977, Gath 1974). These older sisters tended to be most likely to enter a caring profession and to remain involved with their adult sibling, but were also at risk for school failure and stress (Cleveland and Miller 1977). More recent research by Lobato *et al.* (1987) suggests that sisters in the family of a child with a disability experienced more restrictions on social activities than matched controls, and brothers experienced the opposite – more privileges and fewer responsibilities. The research of Stoneman *et al.* (1987, 1988, 1989) found that older sisters were most likely to take on the role of care-giver or manager for the child with special needs in the family. They found that increased child-care responsibilities were associated with increased sibling conflict and less positive sibling interactions. These findings suggest that the nature of a sibling's responsibilities for the child with special needs may add to sibling conflict, and that the allocation of care-giving demands among siblings be considered to make sure that brothers and sisters share these family chores.

Concerns about the future

Finally, siblings experience increasing concerns about their and their siblings' future (Fish and Fitzgerald 1980, Powell and Gallagher 1993). As siblings grow older their worries and concerns about the future naturally increase and become more well-defined. Siblings lacking basic information about the disability will worry about their own ability to have children and the likelihood of having a child with a disability (Parfit 1975). Siblings also worry about their future responsibilities for the child with special needs when they grow up and their parents become unable to care for their brothers and sisters. As one sister noted:

> We all have to worry. Who else is going to be there? I will have to worry and it will be my responsibility; I think about it all the time. I think about the person I am going to marry: when I meet someone, they are not going to just marry me, but they are going to have to love my brother and know he is going to be around all my life.
>
> (Fish 1993)

Fish and Fitzgerald (1980) found that most siblings did not know what future plans their parents had made for their brother or sister, and reported anxiety about how the child would be cared for, and their role in that care. McCullough (1981) reported that the majority of parents in their study had not made plans for the care of their child with special needs, although most of their children assumed that they had made such plans. Others who have studied siblings of children with special needs (Murphy 1979, Parfit 1975, Powell and Gallagher 1993) have urged parents to talk openly about the future with their children and to make plans long before the need is at hand.

Opportunities experienced by brothers and sisters of people with special needs

At the same time that these sibling concerns have become better understood, the opportunities experienced by these brothers and sisters are also being acknowledged (Meyer and Vadasy 1994, Powell and Gallagher 1993, Turnbull and Turnbull 1993).

Appreciation

Siblings often develop a keen appreciation for their own good health and families.

> People tend to think in simplistic terms, not in reality. My mother, for example, is not a saint. In some ways she has still not come to terms with my sister's disability. Yet I see her as a tower of strength. I don't know if I would have that much strength.
>
> (Julie, in Remsberg 1989, p. 3)

> Living with Melissa's handicaps makes me so much more cognizant of my own blessings. She provides a constant reminder

of what life could have been like for me if I had been my parents'
oldest daughter. This encourages me to take advantage of my
mental capacities and to take care of my healthy body.

(Watson 1991, p. 108)

Loyalty and advocacy

Although they may fight at home like other brothers and sisters, many
siblings of people with special needs express a strong sense of loyalty
toward their siblings and families (cf. Matthew's contribution in
Chapter 1). One brother put it this way: 'I'm used to being kind to my
brother and sister, so I'm kind to everybody else. But, if someone starts
a fight, I will fight. I won't put up with anyone teasing Wade or Jolene'
(Morrow 1992, p. 4).

Not surprisingly, many brothers and sisters are brave and convincing
advocates for people with special needs, even at ages when the need to
conform and not 'stand out' would discourage them from doing so.

Melissa also gives me a sense of responsibility to inform others
about the realities of Down syndrome. Although speaking in front
of a class usually makes me literally stop breathing and grow dizzy,
I have faced large groups without fear, arguing the right to life of
babies with Down syndrome.

(Watson 1991, p. 108)

Pride

When siblings witness the day-to-day struggles and challenges their
brothers and sisters contend with, siblings frequently express pride in
their sibling's abilities:

Jennifer has probably achieved more than I have. She's been
through so much. She couldn't even talk when she started school;
now she can, and she can understand others. She's really fulfilling
her potential. I'm not sure the rest of us are.

(Cassie, age 18, in Binkard *et al.* 1987, p. 17)

Maturity

One consequence of the increased responsibilities siblings experience, and the unusual challenges they must face, is the maturity many brothers or sisters develop as a result of successfully coping with a sibling's special needs:

> I have a different outlook on life than many other people my age. I understand that you can't take anything for granted. And you have to be able to look at the positives.... With Jennifer, there are negatives, but there's so much more that is good.
>
> (Andrea, age 19, in Binkard *et al.* 1987, p. 19)

Insights

Finally, as a result of growing up with a brother or sister with special needs a sibling will develop insights on the human condition that are not available to their peers.

> She taught me how to love without reservation; without expectation of returned love. She taught me that everyone has strengths and weaknesses. Martha is no exception. She taught me that human value is not measured with IQ tests.
>
> (Westra 1992, p. 4)

It is important to acknowledge siblings' many unique opportunities, but also to remember that many of these benefits are hard-earned. In this and other ways, siblings' experiences closely parallel their parents' experiences.

Minimising sibling concerns and maximising their opportunities

Within the family, siblings will be likely to spend more time with the child with special needs than any other person, with the exception of the child's mother. And, because the sibling relationship is generally the longest-lasting relationship in the family, brothers and sisters are likely to experience these concerns for a long period of time. Sibling issues are lifespan issues: pre-school-age siblings will grapple with issues their peers do not face, and so will siblings who are senior citizens. Yet many brothers and sisters grow up without resources – such as access to support programmes and sources of information – that would help them in their roles and which many parents now take for granted. The research and clinical literature, along with observations made by siblings themselves, suggest strategies to decrease siblings' concerns and maximise their opportunities.

Provide brothers and sisters with age-appropriate information

Most brothers and sisters have a life-long, and ever-changing, need for information. And parents and service providers have an obligation proactively to provide siblings with helpful information. Agencies representing specific disabilities and illnesses should be challenged to prepare materials specifically for young readers.

Provide siblings with opportunities to meet other siblings of children with special needs

For most parents, the thought of 'going it alone', without the benefit of knowing another parent in a similar situation is unthinkable. Yet this happens routinely to brothers and sisters. Sibshops (Meyer and Vadasy 1994) and similar group meetings offer siblings the same common sense valued by parents. They let brothers and sisters know that they are not alone with their unique joys and concerns.

Encourage good communication with typically developing children

Open and honest communication between parent and child is always a family's goal, and it is especially important in families where there is a child with special needs. An evening course in active listening can help improve communication among all family members. Also, books, such as *How to Talk So Kids Will Listen and Listen So Kids Will Talk,* and *Siblings Without Rivalry* (both by Adele Faber and Elaine Mazlich) provide helpful tips on communicating with children.

Encourage parents to set aside special time to spend with their typically developing children

Children need to know from their parents' deeds and words that their parents care about them as individuals. Parents who carve time out of a busy schedule to grab a bite at a local burger joint or window shop at the mall with their typically developing children convey a message that parents 'are there' for them as well.

Parents and service providers need to learn more about siblings' experiences

Sibling panels, books, newsletters and videos are all excellent means of spreading information about sibling issues. This knowledge will allow both parents and providers to address siblings' concerns proactively.

Encourage parents to reassure their typically developing children by planning for the future of the child with special needs

Early in life, brothers and sisters begin to worry about what obligations they will have towards their sibling in the days to come. Parents should be encouraged to plan for the future and, equally important, share these plans with their children. When brothers and sisters are 'brought into the loop' and given the message that they have their parents' blessing to pursue their dreams, their future involvement with their sibling will be a choice instead of an obligation.

Including brothers and sisters: implications for agencies

Many agencies are beginning to realise that siblings are too valuable to ignore and have begun changing policies and procedures to acknowledge the important roles brothers and sisters play. Here are a few considerations for agencies.

Are siblings included in the agency's definition of 'family'?

Many educational and health care agencies have begun to embrace an expansive definition of families. In the USA, for instance, early intervention programmes for young children with special needs mandate IFSPs and paediatric health programmes aspire to 'family-centered care'. However, providers may still need to be reminded that there is more to a family than the child with special needs and his/her parents.

Organisations that use the word 'parent' when 'family' or 'family member' is more appropriate send a message to brothers and sisters, grandparents and other family members that the programme is not for them. Yet today, siblings and primary care-giver grandparents play increasingly active roles in the lives of people with disabilities.

Does the agency reach out to brothers and sisters?

Parents and agency personnel should consider inviting (but not requiring) brothers and sisters to attend clinic visits and informational, educational and transition planning meetings. Siblings frequently have legitimate questions which service providers are best able to answer. Brothers and sisters also have informed opinions and perspectives and can make positive contributions to the child's team. For instance, if a family desires their child with special needs to attend the local junior high or play football in the cul-de-sac with other neighbourhood children, siblings – because they know the child, the school, the children and the neighbourhood – may be able to offer unique recommendations.

Does the agency educate staff about issues facing brothers and sisters?

Agencies working with people with special needs have an obligation to learn about their clients' families. And siblings, because they will be likely to have the longest-lasting relationship with the person with special needs, should be included. There are several ways for staff to increase their knowledge of sibling issues. A sibling panel can be a powerful way for agency staff to learn more about life as a brother or sister of a person with a disability or chronic illness (for guidelines, *see* Meyer and Vadasy 1994). There is also a growing number of video tapes, books, web pages and newsletters on sibling issues.

Does the agency have brothers and sisters on the advisory board, and policies reflecting the importance of including siblings?

When siblings are invited to serve on the agency's board, they can represent the interests of other siblings. Their inclusion will reflect the agency's concern for the well-being of brothers and sisters. Developing policy based on the important roles played by brothers and sisters will help ensure that their concerns and contributions are a part of the agency's commitment to families.

Does the agency have a programme specifically for brothers and sisters?

Like their parents, brothers and sisters benefit from talking with others in similar situations. Sibshops and other programmes for pre-school, school-age, teen and adult siblings are growing in number. The Sibling Support Project, which maintains a database of over 200 Sibshops and other sibling programmes across the USA, Canada and England, provides technical assistance on creating local programmes for siblings.

Conclusion

Compared to previous generations, today's siblings – both young and adult – will be likely to assume a larger role in the lives of their brothers and sisters with special needs. This is due to at least three converging social phenomena. Firstly, because of advanced medical technologies, people with disabilities are now outliving their parents. This increases the likelihood that brothers and sisters will eventually look after the affairs of their siblings. Secondly, social policies in many countries dictate that people with disabilities live and work in the community. (In previous generations, adults with disabilities frequently lived in institutions and the state assumed an *in loco parentis* role.) Thirdly, these changes occur at a time when many countries face diminishing economic resources. Consequently, it is reasonable to expect that siblings of the baby-boom and post-baby-boom generation will be called upon to be more involved in the lives of the brothers and sisters with disabilities than any previous generation.

Because of their proximity to and long history with their siblings who have special needs, brothers and sisters deserve parents' and providers' attention and respect. It is no longer sufficient to conceptualise 'a family' as the child with special need and his/her parents. Agencies must be proactive in addressing the concerns of young and adult brothers and sisters. And finally, siblings – especially as they approach their adult years – must make their voices heard.

Further information

The Sibling Support Project of Children's Hospital and Medical Center in Seattle, Washington, is pleased to announce SibNet and the 'brand-new' SibKids listservs. SibNet and SibKids are the Internet's only listservs for and about brothers and sisters of people with special health, developmental, and emotional needs.

Both SibKids (for younger brothers and sisters) and SibNet (for older siblings) allow brothers and sisters an opportunity to share information and discuss issues of common interest with their peers from around the world. We hope SibKids and SibNet will also be of interest to parents, service providers and others interested in the well-being of siblings.

For a no-cost subscription and to learn more about SibKids and SibNet, please visit the Sibling Support Project's newly updated web page at http://www.chmc.org/departmt/sibsupp

If you have further questions about SibKids, SibNet or the work of the Sibling Support Project, please contact:

Don Meyer
Sibling Support Project
Children's Hospital and Medical Center
PO Box 5371, CL–09
Seattle, WA 98105–0371

Phone:
+1 206 368 4911; Fax: +1 206 368 4816; email: dmeyer@chmc.org
Website: http://www.chmc.org/departmt/sibsupp
Direct link to SibNet:
http://www.chmc.org/departmt/sibsupp/sibnet.htm
Direct link to SibKids:
http://www.chmc.org/departmt/sibsupp/sibkids1.htm

Chapter 7

Grandparents: part of the family

Brigit Mirfin-Veitch and Anne Bray

Grandparents are traditionally providers of support to parents of young children. During the past decade the grandparent role within families of children with disabilities has received increasing attention. This increase can be attributed to the development of a family systems approach to disability research and early intervention (Bailey and Simeonsson 1988). Adapted from Bronfenbrenner's model of social ecology (Bronfenbrenner 1979), family systems theory has been viewed as a useful method of investigating the effect of a child with a disability on the family unit (Seligman and Darling 1989, Turnbull and Turnbull 1990).

Family systems theory recognises that the family functions as an interconnected unit where all members affect each other (Seligman and Darling 1989). Using family systems theory to investigate issues pertaining to the families of children with disabilities has resulted in researchers broadening their traditional focus. Where the perspective of the mother has dominated disability research in the past, family systems theory has forced recognition of the importance of other family members. Grandparents, along with fathers and siblings, are family members who have been identified as deserving increased research attention (Meyer 1993).

The role of grandparents in families of children with disabilities

Much of the literature relating to the role of grandparents in families of children with disabilities has focused on the support grandparents provide to parents. For the most part, grandparents have been conceptualised as falling into two categories; those who do and those who do not provide practical and/or emotional support to parents. Seligman (1991) identified grandparents as being either stressors or resources to families. Determining whether grandparents provide support has been achieved, almost exclusively, through the analysis of data from parents only.

A significant body of literature has identified grandparents as important sources of support (Beresford 1994, Fewell 1986, Mirfin-Veitch *et al.* 1996, Sandler *et al.* 1995, Sonnek 1986, Vadasy and Fewell 1986). However, despite these positive findings a great deal of research has focused on the stresses and burdens that some grandparents can occasion for parents upon learning of their grandchild's disability (George 1988, Meyer and Vadasy 1986, Seligman and Darling 1989, Simons 1985, Turnbull and Turnbull 1990).

Lack of grandparent support to parents of children with disabilities has been explored almost entirely with reference to grandparents' non-acceptance of their grandchild's disability (Mirfin-Veitch *et al.* 1997). Vadasy (1987) suggested that grandparents see grandchildren as securing their family's future and the diagnosis of a grandchild's disability puts the predictability of their family's future at risk. This interpretation is based on Kivnick's (1983) conceptual framework of grandparenthood which identified five categories representing the meaning of grandparenthood. One of these categories was labelled 'immortality through clan', meaning that grandparents see grandchildren as ensuring their personal immortality by carrying on the family line. This analysis has been forwarded as one explanation for some grandparents' inability to accept a grandchild with a disability.

Other authors have contended that grandparents experience the same series of emotions as parents do upon learning of a child's disability. Being informed that a grandchild has been diagnosed as having a disability can produce strong feelings of anger, grief or denial for some grandparents (Gabel and Kotsch 1981, Meyer 1993). These emotions may threaten grandparents' ability to provide support to parents at a time when they may require it most (Gabel and Kotsch 1981, Meyer 1993, Meyer and Vadasy 1986). Grandparents may also be grieving for their son or daughter's own stress and grief. This experience has been referred to as dual or double grief (Gardner 1996, Meyer and Vadasy 1986, Seligman and Darling 1989, Vadasy *et al.* 1986).

Parents of children with disabilities have been identified as experiencing reduced social networks (Kazak and Marvin 1984). This fact coupled with the evidence that grandparents do provide vital support roles in some families has led to a concentration on how to make grandparents more effective providers of assistance. The negative effect on parents created by grandparents struggling to come to terms with the fact of a grandchild's disability has been well-documented (Gabel and Kotsch 1981, George 1988, Meyer and Vadasy 1986, Seligman and Darling 1989, Simons 1985, Turnbull and Turnbull 1990). Workshops and other similar programmes have been designed to assist grandparents to accept the fact of their grandchild's disability and to provide effective informal support. These workshops provide grandparents with education, information and the opportunity to discuss with peers their feelings and concerns regarding their grandchild. As a result grandparents have come to terms with their grandchild's disability and have become less of a burden and more of a support to the child's parents (Gabel and Kotsch 1981, George 1988, Meyer and Vadasy 1986, Turnbull and Turnbull 1990).

The positive attributes of supportive grandparents have not been explored comprehensively. Some studies have documented the valued and vital support roles that grandparents fulfil in some families (Beresford 1994, Vadasy and Fewell 1986), but these studies have provided little information regarding the specific factors and characteristics that lead to grandparents providing support in a manner that is acceptable to parents. Because failure to provide support has been linked closely with grandparent inability to accept the fact of a child's disability, it has been assumed that grandparents who do provide support do so because they have adjusted better to the fact of their grandchild's disability. Little attention, therefore, has been paid to other issues which may impact on the way grandparents respond or fail to respond to parents' support needs (Mirfin-Veitch *et al.* 1997).

Intergenerational relationships in families with a child with a disability

Mirfin-Veitch *et al.* (1996) discussed the extent and nature of support provided by grandparents to parents of children with disabilities. Two types of parent–grandparent relationships, referred to as 'involved' and 'less involved', were identified. Relationships were classified as 'involved' when grandparents supplied practical and/or emotional support, and as 'less involved' when grandparents did not provide such support to parents (Mirfin-Veitch *et. al.* 1997). The nature of parent–grandparent relationship history emerged as the most significant factor influencing support patterns. Pairs were more successful in dealing with the support needs created by disability if they shared a history of constant grandparent support over various life issues. Those with a 'sporadic' relationship history were found not to experience consistent levels of support. Within these two categories the degree to which support was evident or less evident differed.

The study which these articles report identified factors which were significant in determining whether parent–grandparent relationships would be involved or less involved. The role of grandparents in families of children with disabilities was found to be influenced by variables other than the presence of disability.

Twelve parents and related grandparents of children with disabilities provided data for the study, primarily through participating in in-depth, unstructured qualitative interviews. The perspectives of both parents and grandparents were included to enable the development of a more comprehensive understanding of intergenerational family relationships occurring in families of children with disabilities. Mother–adult daughter combinations comprised nine of the pairs. To our knowledge all participants were of European descent.

In addition to the qualitative interviews, participant diaries collecting quantitative data were incorporated into the design of the study. Diary entries included the number, length and reasons for contacts between parents, grandparents and grandchildren. The data were collected over a four-month period.

Two major themes were identified from analysis of the qualitative interview data. The probability that parents and grandparents would share mutually satisfying and supportive relationships was influenced by the factors and characteristics comprising these two themes. The first theme was generated by the 'sort of family' that parents and grandparents saw themselves as belonging to. The second theme related to the interpersonal relationships existing between adult offspring and their parents or parents-in-law.

'We're that sort of family'

Participants used this phrase frequently to articulate or explain the availability ('We *are* just that sort of family') or lack ('We're *not* that sort of family') of support within their own families.

The 'sort of family' to which involved pairs belonged functioned in a particular manner historically. The traditional functioning of these families did not appear to be altered by the birth or diagnosis of a child with a disability. Unconditional love and acceptance of all family members, frequent extended family contact, and a consistent and shared interpretation of the grandparent role were elements that seemed to be important to the sort of families from which involved pairs derived.

Involved grandparents demonstrated immediate love and acceptance of their grandchild with a disability. It was common for grandparents to provide emotional and practical support from the moment the diagnosis was made. This reaction remained consistent regardless of whether their grandchild's diagnosis was made at birth or months or years after birth. Grandparents did not need a comprehensive understanding of the disability, and its implications, in order to be able to accept the child. Acceptance of the child as a member of the family occurred almost immediately. In a small number of pairs the grandparent had accepted the disability before the parent.

In involved pairs, some grandparents reported feeling sad about their grandchild's disability but this sadness was soon replaced with a 'let's just get on with it' approach. Schell (1981), a parent, reported being appreciative of the fact that grandparents did not immediately burden him with their own grief. Schell contended that this gave him time to get a more stable perspective on his own emotions.

One grandparent described how the extended family had come together after a child had been diagnosed as having a disability soon after birth:

> and it was then that they told us [that grandchild had been diagnosed as having a disability], and, you know, it was such a shock, and we all sat round in a circle and howled ... I suppose we sat round and howled for about 10 days on and off. And that was it. You just got on because [grandchild] was just so lovely.
>
> (Mirfin-Veitch *et al.* 1997)

A grandparent's reaction to the birth of a child with a disability was recounted by a parent: '[Grandparent] just said, "[Grandchild] is a baby, and whatever we need to do, we'll do", and that's basically been it ever since' (Mirfin-Veitch *et al.* 1997).

Grandparents who respond positively to the fact of a grandchild's disability can influence the adjustment of both parents and other extended family members (Vadasy *et al.* 1986, Waisbren 1980). One grandparent recounted a conversation with a parent whose child was subsequently diagnosed as having a disability. In doing so, she illustrated how grandparents can influence family members' responses in the event of a child's disability:

> She said to me, 'I don't know how people cope when people have got disabled children.' And I said, 'Well, you don't – I don't think you even think about it. They are yours and you love them, and then you'll fight and do anything you can for them.'
>
> (Mirfin-Veitch *et al.* 1997)

Grandparent members of involved pairs often developed special relationships with their grandchild with a disability. In providing extensive practical and emotional support to parents, grandparents gained a wonderful understanding of their grandchild. This understanding frequently led to a strong relationship existing between the first and third generation. One grandmother said: 'Oh, I'm closer to [grandchild with disability]. I always say I've got one favourite and seven come second. Because she bonded with me, I'm the one – if [mother] is not about I'm the next in line' (Mirfin-Veitch *et al.* 1997).

Regular extended family contact was an important aspect of the general functioning of the family in involved pairs. General family contact remained at a consistent level despite the presence of a child with a disability in the family. It also appeared that, as well as grandparents, other extended family members could be relied on for support, especially in crises.

> They'll baby-sit and that too ... my youngest brother ... [Child] was in hospital, and I was in there with [child], and I went into labour ... so [brother] actually stayed in hospital with [child] for me.... And between [grandparent] and [brother], they slept there and everything. They were actually wonderful, so no problems with baby-sitting.
>
> (Mirfin-Veitch *et al.* 1997)

Geographical proximity was not found to have a significant impact on the support patterns existing between involved pairs. Even when family members were geographically scattered, the support needs of individual members were met. Conversely, in other less involved pairs the relationships between parents and grandparents, or grandparents and their grandchildren, were not improved by close geographical proximity.

The grandparent role was well-defined within the families of involved pairs. Parents and grandparents held strong and similar views on what it meant to be a grandparent. Nurturing of both the parent and the grandchild was a significant element of the role that grandparents fulfilled. Care and concern was not concentrated solely on the child but also on the well-being of the parent as grandparents recognised the pressures parents sometimes faced. One grandparent articulated this feeling: 'As a grandparent I think my real concern is for the parents rather than the child' (Mirfin-Veitch *et al.* 1997).

Being available to provide support to their family was the element that grandparent members of involved pairs perceived as being most critical to their role. Even when grandparents were still in paid work some continued to see it as their duty to accommodate the support needs of family members. One working grandparent met this demand by taking holidays to coincide with school holidays in order to be able to provide respite for the parent of a child with a disability. In involved pairs, the obligation to family was perceived as taking precedence over all other responsibilities.

Parent members of involved pairs possessed high expectations of grandparents but displayed a reciprocal approach to their relationship. The extensive amounts of support received from some grandparents were accepted and appreciated but parents were concerned that their requests for assistance did not compromise grandparents' ability to enjoy their own interests. Parent members of involved pairs were also more likely to recognise grandparents' own support needs and adjust their requests for assistance accordingly. Adjustment to the tasks that grandparents accomplished occurred progressively as both grandparents and grandchildren got older and the needs and abilities of both parties changed.

In less involved pairs there was no established support pattern either between the parent and grandparent, or the parent and any other extended family member. Reciprocity of support was not a feature of the relationships existing between less involved pairs. Parent members of these pairs often reported feeling dissatisfied with the level of support provided by grandparents but failed to acknowledge that grandparents had their own lives, interests and support needs. A great deal has been documented in the literature regarding how parents feel when grandparents fail to respond to their support needs. Grandparents sometimes need support themselves and feel similarly dissatisfied when parents fail to respond. One grandparent commented on this situation:

And I'm afraid, I mean, no more I can do than that. If she comes, she comes; if she doesn't, we can't be running around. We've got enough worries, as I said. [Spouse] has been home sick for 9 years now, and I've got enough to worry about with him and myself without having to chase around and worry about what [parent] is doing.

(Mirfin-Veitch *et al.* 1997)

Relationship history

The mutual satisfaction that parents and grandparents felt about their current relationship was determined by relationship history more than any other factor. The importance of relationship history emerged from the data as the study progressed and was not a concept that the authors identified as deserving of attention prior to the commencement of the study.

Involved parent–grandparent pairs had experienced, almost without exception, a shared history of positive relations. Grandparents were more able to provide support in a manner that parents found helpful and acceptable if a long-term closeness had previously existed. When a child was diagnosed as having a disability the relationship history between pairs, as well as the 'sort of family' to which they belonged, determined how grandparents would react (Mirfin-Veitch *et al.* 1997).

Two broad characteristics were interpreted as signalling a positive relationship history. A combination of continuity of closeness, and of open and effective communication, were found to be features common to involved parent–grandparent pairs.

Continuity of closeness was defined as being a relationship unbroken by extended periods of conflict. If continuity of closeness had been a feature of the relationship that parent–grandparent pairs had experienced in the past, this pattern was likely to continue regardless of the fact of a child's disability. This finding corresponds with de Vaus (1994) who contended that grandchildren did not transform a troubled parent–adult child relationship, but rather they provided another arena in which the long-term patterns of the relationship were repeated.

The parent members of less involved pairs sometimes perceived the fact of a child's disability as having an effect on the availability of grandparent support. Parents reported that their failure to receive support was due to grandparents' non-acceptance of their grandchild's disability. This interpretation was not supported by the data from grandparents who, in all but one case, had provided extensive support to parents on a number of specific occasions. The fact that parents did not acknowledge this help indicated that continuous rather than spasmodic support was expected.

The relationship already established between less involved parent–grandparent pairs remained unchanged by the presence of a child with a disability. The absence of support appeared to be a reflection of the sporadic or troubled nature of the interpersonal relationships between these parents and grandparents. Disability did, however, exacerbate the level of discontent that parents felt regarding the quality of the relationship they shared with a grandparent. Often parents were feeling a greater need for support and felt let down by the lack of response by grandparents. Despite this need for support, parent members of less involved pairs sometimes actively denied themselves a potential source of informal support because conflict within their relationship defied resolution: 'No I probably wouldn't have let [grandparent] look after [grandchild] because we don't get on particularly well' (Mirfin-Veitch *et al.* 1997).

The resolution of difficulties between parents and grandparents can be achieved only through open and effective communication. Continuous closeness is more likely to be a feature of a relationship when members enjoy good communication. Evidence of communication fraught with misinterpretation and misunderstanding was common in less involved pairs. In some situations misunderstanding or communication breakdown had the potential to result in the cessation of support. The spasmodic relationship history that many less involved pairs shared suggested that reinstatement of grandparent provision had the potential to occur but the time frame within which it did so was variable.

Parent members of both involved and less involved pairs valued highly grandparents' ability to be able to be perceptive of the needs of parents. Developing an accurate perception of the parents' support needs was difficult for the grandparent members of less involved pairs. Being perceptive of the parent's needs was complex when a problematic relationship history had reduced both members' ability to communicate effectively. Parents resented the fact that grandparents had to be alerted verbally to their need for support. Lack of established patterns of communication between parents and grandparents also had the effect of rendering parents incapable of asking for assistance: 'It hurt. It hurt me terribly because I really needed help and didn't know how to ask for it' (Mirfin-Veitch *et al.* 1997).

The lack of communication within less involved pairs was in contrast to the climate of open communication within which involved parent–grandparent pairs generally interacted. Requesting support from grandparents was comfortable for parents as they felt that grandparents were non-judgemental. The trust that was present in the relationships existing between involved pairs made it easy for parents to make specific requests for assistance. Continuous closeness, and open and effective communication in the parent–grandparent relationship, allowed grandparents to understand instinctively the support tasks that the parent would most appreciate. Parents valued grandparents relieving them of the need always to have to ask for help.

All grandparents had a fear of being perceived as interfering. Activities undertaken by grandparents classified as involved were rarely perceived by the parent members of these pairs as interference. Grandparent members of involved pairs remained aware of negotiating the invisible boundary within which behaviour is defined as supportive rather than interfering. The advantage of having a history of positive relations meant the grandparents were successful in achieving this balance.

Parent members of less involved pairs were frequently critical of the fact that they were not receiving grandparent support. This corresponds with Hornby and Ashworth's (1994) finding that parents expressed dissatisfaction with grandparent lack of support if the failure to provide assistance was linked to grandparent disinterest or to poor relationships between family members.

The notion that availability of support may be related to factors pertaining to disability may be valid for some families. For many families, however, factors unrelated to disability clearly influence support patterns and deserve greater consideration. If parents and grandparents belong to a certain 'sort of family' and share a positive relationship history, support is likely to have been, and to remain, a feature of their relationship regardless of the presence of a child with a disability. The fact of a child's disability is not likely to challenge a previously involved parent–grandparent relationship or to transform a formerly less involved association. Acknowledging that factors independent from disability can determine the level of support in families of children with disabilities serves to de-emphasise a pathology view of disability, which attributes all family problems to the presence of a child with a disability (Turnbull *et al.* 1986).

Grandparent workshops are one method of encouraging and supporting informal support within some families. The factors hindering provision of support in other families, however, may render this approach ineffective. It is important to find alternative strategies to promote positive relationships and informal support within families.

Implications for early intervention services

Acknowledgement that support patterns within the extended family are often determined by factors other than those related to disability has implications for several areas of professional practice, and supports a family-focused approach to early intervention.

Professionals working with parents at the time a child is diagnosed as having a disability need to be aware of the nature of intergenerational relationships existing in particular families. By undertaking a wider assessment of the family, professionals could, at an early stage, encourage a level of involvement by grandparents (or other extended family members) that is acceptable and useful to parents. Involving grandparents in the delivery of information regarding a child's disability may be an accommodation welcomed by parents. Encouraging grandparents to access information regarding their grandchild's disability may alleviate any pressing fears regarding the effect of the disability or related health concerns. Parents are also relieved of the task of relaying this information to other family members. By creating an environment that is receptive of grandparents and other extended family members a pattern of support between parents and grandparents can be encouraged and supported.

Involving grandparents in this manner would be uncomplicated if grandparents and parents belonged to a particular 'sort of family' and shared a positive relationship history. Encouraging the provision of support would be more difficult if parents and grandparents displayed a history of problematic relations where support was not characteristic of their relationship. In this case, interventions of a more formal nature might need to be implemented. The promotion of family functioning and intergenerational relationships may need to be the focus of interventions. Interventions will need to be more comprehensive and responsive to individual families as the issues negatively impacting on provision of support will differ and may be long-standing.

The initial step in the creation of effective networks of informal support within families may be assisted through the promotion of relationship counselling to address long-standing issues that impede the relationships existing between some parents and grandparents. Relationships experienced by adults and their parents or parents-in-law receive little practical attention. Resolving issues impeding the exchange of support within families becomes critical when there is a greater need for support as is often the case for families of children with disabilities.

The omission of grandparents from parents' informal support networks may impact also on the grandchild with a disability and other children in the family. Grandparent provision of support to families of children with disabilities need not be measured only in terms of the emotional and practical support they offer to parents. Grandparents also provide support to their grandchild with a disability by displaying the qualities of acceptance, interest and patience. Other children in the family benefit from attention received from their grandparent and learn from the positive behaviour modelled by supportive grandparents.

Modifying professional practice in order to encourage the involvement of already supportive grandparents or trying actively to assist parents and grandparents to resolve issues that are eliminating support from being a part of their relationship, may work for some families. However, for other families establishing a situation where grandparent provision of support can be relied upon may be impossible. For families in this position formal support must be available. Policy changes which reduce the level of formal support available to families can create a situation where greater pressure is placed on informal networks. In families where informal support is not available at all, reduction in formal services has the potential to cause severe stress for the family unit.

Implications for future research

The level of importance placed by parents of children with disabilities on support from grandparents suggests that future research should explore methods of strengthening family relations and support networks within families. It is also important that methods of assessment of families' needs for formal support services are designed to take into account their access to acceptable informal supports from extended family members.

The reported study was based on a small sample of participants. Further research to investigate and expand on issues raised by this research needs to be conducted. Acknowledgement of the gender bias apparent in the current study sample, where mother–adult daughter combinations were by far the most common pairings, also must be made. Earlier findings may provide an explanation for this situation. Marks and McLanahan (1993) found that mothers dominate social support relationships and are involved in both the giving and receiving of social support. de Vaus (1994) discovered that relationships between mothers and daughters were closer, more intense and more demanding than relationships between parents and sons. Contemporary research ethics required that parents and grandparents chose to be involved in the study and thus may have possessed strong feelings about their relationship at the time of interview.

Specific areas to explore in future studies include the relationship between the age and employment status of grandparents. Both these factors have the potential to make a significant impact on how support patterns in families change over time and could help facilitate the planning of formal services designed to meet the support requirements for families of children with disabilities.

Part III: Cultural perspectives

Chapter 8

Early intervention education services in Aotearoa/New Zealand: inclusion of young infants and young children in regular early childhood education settings – current provisions, issues and challenges[1]

Dee Twiss, Beverley Stewart and Maureen Corby

Introduction

Free and compulsory education has been provided in Aotearoa/New Zealand for around 120 years. However, until recently, legal responsibility for a suitable education for children with significant disabilities remained the responsibility of parents. This remains the case for children under five years of age. Nevertheless, while not yet a legal right, increasingly comprehensive early intervention provisions are now available.

This chapter sets out to describe:

- early provisions for infants and young children with special developmental needs;
- current early intervention services in Aotearoa/New Zealand;
- issues and challenges in achieving excellent family-focused early intervention services.

Very early provision was made for the education of children with sensory disabilities, such as the establishment of educational programmes for deaf and blind children.[2] From the early twentieth century some provision was made for children with mild learning needs, and from 1917 significant provisions were developed for children with mild to severe levels of disability, particularly intellectual, through a wide range of special education options within segregated special schools, special education units or classes within regular schools, or through access to additional support within regular classes. Nevertheless, legal responsibility for education of children with major disabilities remained with parents. Education and 'training' provisions for children with very severe or profound intellectual disability were available through a parent-driven voluntary agency funded jointly by public donation and social welfare state funding, or within-state-funded psychopaedic hospitals supporting multi-profoundly disabled persons from birth onwards.

It was not until the 1989 Education Act that Aotearoa/New Zealand extended a legal right to education to *all* children from the age of five years, with compulsory attendance for all children from six years, within state schools of their parents' choice. 'People who have Special Educational Needs (SEN) (whether because of disability or otherwise) have the same rights to enrol and receive education at state schools as people who do not' (Education Act 1989). Under this law, children with disabilities aged 5 to 21 years have access to the same educational provisions as their peers and must be enrolled in a state-registered school. Parents who wish to home-school their children may have their alternative curriculum accepted by the Ministry of Education (MOE) if the education programme to be offered is seen to be equivalent to that offered within the state school system.

Currently, although children younger than five years of age do not have a legal right to education services, the Aotearoa/New Zealand government contributes in a major way to the many early education provisions available through national services, trusts, parent cooperatives and individually owned early childhood education centres. Successive governments have been increasingly committed to the provision of early intervention services for infants and young children with special developmental needs, and to the provision of these in the most inclusive way that can meet the individual child's needs.

Early provisions

Although non-compulsory early childhood education provision had existed since the turn of the century through kindergartens, and from the 1940s with the Playcentre Movement (a parent cooperative educational programme), education sector involvement in early childhood special education was practised only very tentatively throughout the first half of this century. Provision of services depended very much on the area in which a family lived. Some areas had notable services, while others, particularly those in rural areas, had none. Most infants and young children with disabilities remained at home, were institutionalised within hospital settings or were fortunate enough to attend educational services for infants and young children with intellectual disabilities provided by voluntary organisations, such as the

New Zealand Society for the Intellectually Handicapped (IHC).[3]

Over the period that the IHC was a lead agency in pre-school special education service provision it was rethinking its philosophies and policies as international opinion turned increasingly towards the values of normalisation, least restrictive environment and main-streaming/integration/inclusion. In the early 1980s, IHC advocated vigorously for an amendment to the 1964 Education Act to rid it of the clauses which 'discriminated against children who are severely handicapped' and applauded the 'growing support provided by the Education Department for an increasing number of intellectually disabled youngsters being integrated into normal schools' (Annual report of the IHC 1982). Also during the 1980s there occurred a gradual transfer of responsibility from health and welfare to the education sector for educational provision for even the most profoundly disabled infants and young children.

By 1986 in Aotearoa/New Zealand, support for integration of all pre-school children was openly advocated. In 1987, a Draft Review of Special Education was prepared. This review noted some issues of concern in the then delivery of early intervention services. These concerns (Brown 1989) included:

- access: variable throughout the country;
- programmes categorical in nature and children being labelled at an early age;
- need for better service coordination.

The points were well made. Early intervention services, where available at all, were provided in a loosely linked multidisciplinary manner whereby a variety of specialist staff individually assessed the child and focused on programme delivery aspects related to their own professional perspective. While informed liaison was always a goal, the focus on the individual child and the lack of cohesion between the separate programmmes did not provide a family-focused approach to early intervention. Consequently families faced many issues including: involvement with too many professionals at any one time; unco-ordinated service delivery between services; differing and frequently conflicting advice; and unilateral decision-making on the part of many professionals.

In 1989, during major educational restructuring,[4] the 'Before Five' Special Education Working Group (Twiss 1989) was set up to include individuals from a wide range of early childhood facilities, voluntary agencies, parents, special education professionals and tertiary training institutions. The group alerted the government to research on the effects of educational intervention experiences at particular developmental levels. Their report noted particularly the developmental synchrony in the learning of many physical, social, emotional, thinking and language concepts which provide a base for later learnings, and took the stance that the impact of special attention is therefore greatest when it is provided at the earliest time in a child's life and within the child's usual home, community and educational setting. Comprehensive proposals for early childhood special education administrative structures, professional practices and processes were developed, with an overall recommendation 'that the special education service in early childhood education provide a unified needs-based service, free and accessible for all whānau of families of infants and young children with special needs, within their own community' (Twiss 1989). In October 1989, the Special Education Service was established throughout Aotearoa/New Zealand. This organisation's early intervention policy set out to implement the new government requirements and emphasised:

- planned coordinated early intervention services for infants and young children with special developmental needs, based on established good practices as confirmed by research and international understandings;
- systems for early identification;
- parents as essential decision-makers within the team for their child;
- family-focused services delivered to the child through needs-based and regularly reviewed Individual Development Plans (IDP);
- inclusion of children with special developmental needs within the context of their families and community education settings;
- services available from birth until the child is settled within the school system;
- ongoing availability of specialist staff working collaboratively across disciplines and across agencies to provide a range of service provisions including transdisciplinary teams;
- integrated service provision through collaboration with other voluntary and state agencies supporting the family;
- contestable funding within a limited discretionary resource available to all service providers;
- discretionary resource allocation for individual children, determined by IDP process, ensuring equitable, effective and efficient resource usage;
- well-developed accountability processes.

The development and implementation of area-wide early

intervention plans and coordination with health sector child development teams were considered a priority in order to provide services in a cohesive and equitable manner, regardless of the funding source.

Current early intervention provisions in education

Developmental benefits of early intervention for the child and family, and substantial cost benefits for the state, have been readily accepted in Aotearoa/New Zealand with significant government funds going to both health and education sectors. Health sector early intervention funding is focused on the provision of occupational and physical therapies. There are a few major trusts providing general early intervention services and others emphasising specific interventions, for example, the Conductive Education Trust.

Current government aims for special education resourcing in the early childhood sector for the next few years are:

> to promote the social, emotional, intellectual and physical growth of young children to take maximum advantage of their potential for learning; to prevent the development of secondary disabilities in young children with developmental problems and to support the families of such young children to enable them to meet the needs of their children as effectively as possible on an ongoing basis.
>
> (Twiss 1996)

Because Specialist Education Services is the national education-based early intervention lead agency, the focus here will be on the implementation of its national policies in early intervention.

Specialist staff

Specialist Education Services staff involved in providing early intervention services include area advisers (early intervention),[5] psychologists, speech language therapists, early intervention teachers,[6] advisers for deaf children,[7] kaitakawaenga[8] and paraprofessionals called education support workers.[9] Early intervention teachers were a new initiative in 1988 with five appointments across the country. There are now over 120 part- and full-time positions.

Early identification and early intervention

Specialist Education Services areas have developed 'child find' protocols encouraging early referrals to support parents, whãnau[10] and other care-givers at the critical periods of identification of special developmental needs in order to maximise appropriate child development and minimise secondary problems. Timely referral would be easier to achieve if it were possible to specify the characteristics of infants and families most needing early intervention support. However, current research shows that in identifying, defining and assessing risk factors, neither child factors in themselves, nor isolated environmental factors provide highly reliable predictive information. In other words, selecting infants by means of specific disability or environmental category has not proved to be an effective way of identifying children most needing and benefiting from early intervention services (Moore 1990). Therefore a holistic perspective which takes into consideration a cluster of child, family and environmental factors is needed.

The issues of accessibility and equity also make it important that information is available to parents as well as educators in a variety of formats and languages (through brochures and videos, for example). Referrals may be made by any concerned person. Informed parental consent is essential, and centralised referral processes ensure prioritisation of referrals and timely pick-up by the appropriate team members. There has been a progressive move towards referral at a younger age and in some rural areas over 50 per cent of referrals relate to children less than two years of age.

Parents as decision-makers

Specialist Education Services recognises that the development of children is best enhanced through involvement with persons with whom the child has established 'a mutual and enduring attachment' (Bronfenbrenner 1990). Specialist Education Services respects the determination of families to make decisions on their own behalf and works to support the ability of the family to support their own child through:

- enhancing a sense of community;
- mobilising resources and supports;
- shared responsibility and collaboration;
- protecting family integrity;
- strengthening family functioning;
- proactive and innovative service practices.

(Dunst 1990)

Family-focused support is evidenced through case work where parents are essential decision-makers and through the opportunities provided for mutual support between parents, information and skills exchange that have developed. Some areas provide for this in deliberate ways, such as including parents on staff appointment panels, and through parent forums which provide excellent opportunities for parent input into current practice, policy and professional development at a local and national level. Nationally parents are represented on the Board with overall responsibility for Specialist Education Services.

Service delivery

A continuum of services and provisions is needed, with systems that are flexible, accessible and responsive to meet the changing developmental needs of the family. Through Specialist Education Services, a range of services is provided, including specialist assessment, programme planning and development, advice and support, service coordination and hands-on direct teaching, therapy and support. This may be provided by a case team or by individual members of a team. Specialist Education Services, early intervention teams try to include culturally competent staff acceptable to the families they work with. Maori staff members will be consulted where a referral is received from a Maori family, either as keyworker for the family or as a consultant to the team.

Where possible Specialist Education Services early intervention teams work in a transdisciplinary team manner (Doyle this volume, Landerholm 1990). This approach involves members of the case team in joint assessment of needs, programme development and evaluation. Roles and responsibilities are shared by team members and, where possible and appropriate for the child, the team member most acceptable to the family acts as the keyworker in programme implementation, so that the family do not always need to see many different specialists. Family members are increasingly sharing this keyworker role with professionals.

Inclusion in early childhood education centres is further facilitated by additional direct support of individual children through education support workers supervised directly by early intervention teachers for about 2,000 young children with two or more major developmental needs, within their educational setting (0.06 per cent of the child population). This paraprofessional support is highly valued by parents and teachers. In employing education support workers, who work directly with the child, serious effort is made to match the culture of the family involved.

Inclusive services

The right to be part of the community, including the right to be educated alongside one's peers, is part of a wide international movement recognising the rights of disabled people. Educational research and practice demonstrates that learners with special developmental needs benefit from playing and learning alongside agemates in appropriately resourced regular settings. It is also regularly observed that the inclusion of children with special needs in these settings is beneficial for other children and for the wider community. By including the child in neighbourhood community centres, the parents and whānau are included as well.

By far the majority of young children (well over 95 per cent) with mild to very profound developmental needs are able to be supported within regular community early childhood education settings. For a very few[11] with major and complex needs, support can also be provided within specialist facilities such as special day schools for physically disabled children, one of the five Conductive Education Programmes available nationwide, the two major resource schools for deaf children or services provided by the national Vision Education Centre, as well as distance education support from the Correspondence School.

Te Whāriki curriculum plans

For each child an individualised plan is prepared in order to provide for this child's inclusion within the Te Whāriki Early Childhood curriculum.[12] The process is family-focused with ecological assessments and planning meetings that include care-givers as essential and active decision-makers on their child's behalf. Assessment is likely to involve direct observation, developmental and judgement-based appraisals and a synthesis of information from a wide variety of sources including the family and others involved. Assessment most often occurs in the family home and/or early childhood centre, wherever the child's behaviour provides the most valid and reliable picture of what is really happening. The focus of the assessment process is oriented towards current skills assessment as well as preferred learning modes in order to provide learning objectives that are developmentally and functionally appropriate, and embedded within the regular early childhood curriculum.

Te Whāriki individual planning meetings include those with a significant knowledge of the child as well as advocates and others determined by the family and whānau. The meeting works to achieve consensus on the child's current skills and further learning objectives, and also any goals that will support the family. The early intervention team is there to encourage and support them as their child's prime educators while avoiding the expectation that parents are to be their child's 24-hours-a-day teachers.

The overall programme is planned to be child-centred, child-initiated and play-based, with incidental teaching embedded within the child's natural social contexts providing opportunities for both structured and spontaneous meaningful learning. This is not to say that a stimulating environment in itself is progressive. Rather, personalised stimulation and programming fitted specifically for that child and his/her care-givers, in natural settings, is likely to challenge both child and care-giver towards the development of cooperative reciprocal behaviours and therefore further learning encounters which can be generalised.

The family and the keyworker will also plan carefully for transitions into the school sector. Transition can be an extremely complex time for parents as it involves significant challenges in terms of attitudes towards integration within regular programmes, changes in professional support, in terms of time and process, together with the need to build up new support networks in the community.

Cross-agency teamwork

Across the country Specialist Education Services early intervention teams try to work closely with health sector teams which employ physiotherapists, occupational therapists and social workers, and with the paediatricians who work with young children with disabilities. In most areas the education and health teams now work in collaborative case teams to plan shared cases.

Accountability

A comprehensive and national evaluation of the functioning of the early intervention teams was undertaken in 1992. This included a survey of 30 per cent of Special Education Service parent consumers. While recording a very high level of overall satisfaction, parents commented on a need for higher staff levels, on high case loads, and issues relating to continuity of particular skilled personnel such as speech-language therapists. Many would have welcomed earlier referral to teams, and some sought more active involvement in the assessment and programming process for their child. This feedback was carefully considered in the further development of services within the Specialist Education Services.

Since 1992, annual national randomised surveys involving parents and early childhood education settings have confirmed a consistently high level of satisfaction of at least 95 per cent. Nevertheless, by 1995 some early intervention teams sought feedback at critical points of the intervention process: that is, at assessment, programme implementation and evaluation. This would provide information on independent variables such as child characteristics at entry, family demographics, family ecology, programme variables and other services involved, as well as child and family outcome variables. This framework for evaluation of intervention efficacy is based on the recommendations of Marfo and Dinero (1991).

Since 1995 review schedules aimed at facilitating best practice in early intervention have been trialled. From 1997, a much more comprehensive approach is being implemented nationally through national service performance protocols, standards and measures for the specialist services provided.

Challenges in further development

Current challenges to excellent service provision in early intervention relate to:
- structural and organisational issues – socio-political and resourcing;
- service delivery issues – client- and family-focus, individualised plans and inclusion within the early childhood curriculum, play-based, child-centred programmes;
- staff issues – providing for cultural diversity, tertiary training and ongoing availability of appropriately skilled staff within transdisciplinary teams.

Structural issues

Socio-political issues
Over the last ten years the community has been grappling with two, sometimes parallel sometimes mutually antagonistic, ideologies. As a result policies have been formed with overlapping perspectives: for example, the medical and charity models, and the rights discourse. The latter argues for educational opportunities comparable with those enjoyed by other sectors of society. During the 1980s there were some landmark shifts relating to community provisions for people with disabilities. The 1989 Education Act, guaranteeing every child the right to an education, rejected an adherence to a deficit model of disability. Brown (1994b) discusses the effects of the 1990s political climate's clear movement towards a libertarian right ideology, the freedom of the 'possessive individual' and the market place. Within libertarian right ideology, state intervention does not necessarily result in greater equity, is unnecessary and should be severely curtailed. Education fulfils the individual, and s/he must pay for that. This assumes that society is a level playing field. Those advocating for individual rights argue that it isn't. There are intrinsic problems for marginalised groups: those who are disabled; those who are poor. Compensatory provision of generalised parenting programmes, focused towards at-risk groups, may be intended to provide support, but arguably do not address the issues of poverty and underprivilege which undermine parents' ability to meet their own children's needs.

As Brown continues, 'possessive individual' theories 'fit uneasily with special education' and other socio-community responsibilities for marginalised groups: 'The issue of devolving power to community level yet allowing equity to be preserved in a market driven economy is the dilemma.' Advisory, regulatory and delivery functions have been separated, and accountability and community responsibility dispersed.

Resourcing issues
The government's general social policy direction has been towards a funder/provider split, contestable funding and devolution of management responsibility for service provision to the local community level. In the area of early intervention services, however, as in some other areas, it resources a national special education crown agency, in recognition of the need to guarantee nationwide access to co-ordinated services. Four regional health authorities also purchase early intervention services. Independent community-initiated early

intervention providers seek funds from both the health and education sectors. This has led to an overlap of some services as well as competition for limited funds between services which need to co-operate to ensure excellent service provision for families.

Overall funding available for early intervention services in New Zealand has increased considerably over the past few years. Successive governments accept international opinion that early intervention works.[13] Nevertheless the resource available to the early childhood education sector remains proportionally far less than that available to the school sector.

In Aotearoa/New Zealand it has been difficult to achieve agreement concerning the funding of specialist education services. The key questions surround whether funds should be maintained in one pool and dispersed according to needs-based priorities but 'controlled by experts', thereby disempowering local community decision-making, or whether these very limited funds should be divided equally and, as a consequence, thinly between all educational facilities. There is little to suggest that the incidence of children with special needs is distributed in that way.

Service delivery issues

Child find
Client numbers increase each year with greater community awareness of the value of early intervention, and correspondingly earlier identification for services. In addition, current immigration patterns seem to result in a higher proportion of families with children with complex needs seeking support, particularly in large metropolitan areas. These factors increase pressure on already stretched services whose rate of growth is controlled not only by funding but by availability of specialist staff for the team approaches accepted as good practice.

Family focus
As always, achieving effective family-focused services is a challenge. Yet active and sensitive support for families as the most important decision-makers for their children is a paramount goal in providing effective early intervention services and attitude change among professionals. The partnerships between parents and professionals, increasingly evident in case work, now need to be reflected

consistently in ongoing consultation, policy determination, evaluation, staff selection and professional development at every level of interaction. The power of parents to influence political change is acknowledged and needs encouragement and support from professionals. Priorities for action and advocacy must, however, remain firmly driven by parents.

The alignment of Individualised Plans with regular early childhood curriculum

A further challenge relates to ensuring that services maintain a holistic early childhood, rather than 'special education', focus, and that needs-based individual programmes are well-embedded within the regular early childhood curriculum. The new Aotearoa/New Zealand national early childhood education curriculum, Te Whariki, specifies principles relating to:

- Whãkamana – empowerment;
- Kotahitanga – holistic development;
- Whanau-tangata – family and community inclusion;
- Ngã Hononga – responsive relationships.

The curriculum emphasises the cultural influences on learning and the multidirectional nature of early learning: a 'weaving' rather than a 'steps and stairs' learning progression. It emphasises too the holistic nature of learning, and rejects processes that separate a child from its peers.

The emergence of this curriculum re-awakens the international debate surrounding early childhood curriculum-based programming and traditional special education direct teaching programmes. For early interventionists the challenge then is in ensuring that sophisticated needs-based teaching and therapies do reach the child. While these should indeed be embedded within the regular curriculum, programme modifications or additional needed resources are by definition required for the child with special developmental needs.

Play-based child-directed programming versus structured programmes

A further challenge to the early childhood curriculum relates to a recurring trend towards formal instruction in academic skills in early childhood education (as discussed by David, Herbert and Moir this volume), as commercial competition between providers in this sector increases. This emphasis on academic instruction is based on misconceptions about early learning (Elkind 1986, 1987) and is incompatible with curricula based on developmentally appropriate practice (Bredekamp 1987) within overall programmes that are child-centred and child-initiated. Despite few, if any, beneficial positive effects resulting from such approaches, some parents can be easily convinced that they are providing their children with an advantaged early start.

Staffing issues

Mirroring cultural diversity
Early intervention service providers face a tremendous challenge in achieving a personnel mix that adequately represent the many cultures within the client population. Until new graduates in specialist fields mirror community ethnicities, providing parents with the choice of support from people of their culture is not achievable. In particular Specialist Education Services is endeavouring to meet such responsibilities by enhancing bicultural services with the indigenous people, the Tangata Whenua or Maori, and by initiating new Maori for Maori services inclusive of Maori leaders and consultants at national and regional levels to manage the development of these services. In addition, there is planned appointment and enhancement of professional development of Maori staff.

Ongoing availability of essential specialist staff
It is accepted that parents are their child's most significant long-term teacher, 'whereby the development of the child is enhanced through involvement in progressively more complex patterns of reciprocal, contingent interactions with [these] persons with whom the child has established a mutual and enduring attachment' (Bronfenbrener 1990).

In consideration of the training of professionals working in early intervention teams there are major challenges in relation to tertiary training provisions and organisational planning to ensure the ongoing availability of staff from the discipline groups required for effective interdisciplinary and transdisciplinary teaming. Anne Smith *et al.* (1995) emphasise that training is a key component of quality and is more, not less, important for those working with young children, since the children are at a particularly vulnerable stage in their development. All the research shows that the kinds of interactions they have with adults have a profound influence on their development.

There is a range of providers, requirements and training emphases in early childhood education, and the early intervention focus is extremely variable across discipline groups. Such a diverse range of training providers and course content has presented the coherent development of integrated health and education provision of early intervention with the following issues and challenges:

1. Training occurs within each discipline rather than across disciplines, although not only the literature on early intervention but also field reality emphasises the need for a team and an ecological systems approach, because of the complex and interrelated needs of young children with disabilities.

2. The principles and practices of early intervention are given scant attention in most discipline training as opposed to: early childhood development and specialist knowledge in disability (e.g. visual or hearing impairment); particular developmental areas (e.g. physiotherapy, occupational therapy, speech language therapy); or a generic special education problem analysis emphasis (e.g. educational psychologist training).

3. Currently, in Aotearoa/New Zealand only the Diploma in Early Intervention teacher course promotes in-depth study of a systems approach to involvement with families and early childhood development, specifically relating to early intervention principles and practices.

4. Differing theoretical bases direct the training of various disciplines. These include, for example:
   (i)   specialist as opposed to problem analysis approaches;
   (ii) diagnostic as opposed to assessment, intervention and evaluation approaches;
   (iii) deficit as opposed to asset models of disability;
   (iv) child focus as opposed to ecological focus.

5. Developing a team approach across disciplines presents some difficulty with professionals coming from differing theoretical and practice perspectives.

6. For many disciplines there may be minimal involvement with early intervention teams during training in terms of practical and field experience.

7. The level of funding available to course participants may affect the calibre of those moving into early intervention. This is particularly pertinent where substantive experience as a teacher is related to course entry.

Conclusion

New Zealand's early intervention providers, whether education or health based, are succeeding well in their goal of supporting parents through the provision of comprehensive and inclusive early intervention services within regular community settings. Much more rarely, children are supported in centre-based programmes where the parents have preferred this option for their child. Government funding has increased markedly over the past five years in recognition of agreement on the importance of early childhood learning.

The transdisciplinary approach (as discussed by Doyle this volume) that has clear benefits for early intervention team functioning requires changes in individual professional behaviour which is difficult to achieve, even when the professionals understand the goals and accept the challenge. These teams develop over time and require steadfast organisational support that is hard to maintain during repeated restructuring.

Specialist Education Services is currently confirming that transdisciplinary teaming is essential, and is establishing national 'best practice' performance protocols to support the ongoing development of the core specialist early intervention services. These protocols define key services and processes, while providing for service flexibility, local variations and developments.

Schofield (1991) says the level of staff involvement in the development and implementing standards for practice is a predictor of the level of the implementation of those standards. Specialist Education Services is accepting the challenge of involving its staff in the development of these specialist service protocols, recognising also, with Bronfenbrenner (1979), that care-givers' capacity to provide high-quality, responsive and stimulating environments for children is dependent on how the care-givers themselves are cared for.

As well as individual professional and intra-team training and quality standards, interagency coordination clearly requires active and ongoing support. Providing for integrated service delivery through effective, functional cross-agency collaboration remains complex and, even when achieved, is hard to sustain (Fyffe 1995).

The most important challenge of all, is the further involvement of parents and families at all levels of service delivery, thereby putting real meaning into the often used phrase, 'parent–professional partnership'.

Notes

1. This chapter is based on a paper first presented by Dee Twiss and Yvonne Lyons, Principal, Sommerville Special School, at the 10th Annual congress of IASSID at Helsinki in July 1996.
2. Sumner School for Deaf, the world's first state-funded school for deaf children, was established in 1880.
3. The IHC was established in 1949 by a small group of parents dissatisfied with the way their children were being treated by public health authorities and health and education professionals.
4. The government's 'Tomorrows Schools' restructuring in 1989 made major changes in education provision, considerably increasing local community responsibility and input to schools' management.
5. Area advisers (early intervention) are responsible for the development and coordination of high quality early intervention services in their area. They have a particular brief for cross-agency cooperation.
6. Experienced early childhood teachers with additional training in working with children with special needs.
7. Teachers of deaf children with further specialist postgraduate training in the support of families with deaf infants and young children.
8. Maori advisers.
9. Staff without formal training who work with a given child with supervision from the early childhood education centre staff and an early intervention teacher keyworker.
10. 'Whānau': Maori term for a concept approximating to the English phrase 'close and extended family group'.
11. Less than 200 nationally.
12. Aotearoa/New Zealand adopted in 1996 a comprehensive national early childhood curriculum.
13. For example Western States Technical Assistance Resource (WESTAR) published data in 1981 which showed that the cumulative cost of special education for children from birth to 18 years of age was lower on average the earlier resourcing was provided. That is, the total cost of special education on average per child is less than 70 per cent of the total cost if commenced at six years.

Chapter 9

Working with familes in a multi-ethnic European context: implications for services

Fernando Almeida Diniz

Introduction

The focus of this chapter is on the interaction of ethnic minority families with the special education system. An understanding of the dynamics involved is crucial for two main reasons. There is considerable concern at international level about the representation of children of ethnic minority origin in special education. A study in seven European countries found a significantly higher number of ethnic minorities (especially bilingual and Muslim pupils) in special education, mainly because mainstream schools had failed to address their bilingual and bicultural needs (Organisation for Economic Cooperation and Development (OECD) 1987). Secondly, ethnic minority communities have long been cast in a deficit light by mainstream institutions. Their legitimate hopes and aspirations for equal opportunities within the EU have been frustrated not only by overt racism, manifested in harassment and violence, but more significantly by the persistent and widespread racial discrimination which they encounter in securing their rights to public services as families (McEwen 1995). As will be illustrated here, while Europe is multiracial and multi-ethnic in composition, the models underpinning public services remain firmly monocultural, e.g. rarely are issues of *ethnicity* an integral feature of mainstream research and policy. Yet, to ignore these realities is to deny the sources of the barriers ethnic minorities face and the means by which service providers can put in place more effective measures to support them.

In the first section of the chapter, I briefly outline what is known about the societal context within which ethnic minorities presently live in the EU. Next, a review of current research focusing on special education and ethnic minority families in Britain is presented. The third section reports the outcomes of a research study conducted by Diniz and Pal (1997) in Scotland, giving preference to the voice of parents themselves. Finally, I will offer some priorities to guide policy-makers and practitioners who are committed to improving practice in this area.

An analysis of the societal context of ethnic minorities in the EU

Insiders or outsiders?

The term 'ethnic minorities' is problematic as a concept and in the way that it is often used; it came into use since the 1950s to denote immigrant communities with origins in Africa, Asia, Central and South America. A critical feature of this development is that the ethnicity of the new minorities is seen to contrast with that of dominant indigenous European groups in respect of cultural identity, race, colour, language and creed, particularly Islam. It would be more accurate to represent this classification as racialised minorities, who are perceived as visibly different and separate from a stereotyped norm of a European identity; in effect, they are what I prefer to call the 'outsiders'. Just as the classification of 'immigrant' is becoming increasingly irrelevant as a description when applied to the descendants of minority settlers, continued use by policy-makers of a single category of 'ethnic minorities' masks very real differences that exist between and within groups in terms of cultural identity, language, creed and history of settlement, in addition to issues of class, gender and disability.

Social inclusion or exclusion?

There is extensive evidence to demonstrate that ethnic minorities have borne the full force of various ideological shifts within individual states in the EU; the restructuring and resegregation of work, inadequate legal protection, poor housing and welfare have had a disproportionate impact on the life chances of minority families. At the heart of the matter is the racism they experience in their interactions with the institutions of the state (Council of Europe 1991, Ford 1991). Despite this, there has been a reluctance to accept the necessity for change in the legal framework to outlaw racial discrimination, but there are now calls for more comprehensive anti-discrimination legislation, thus:

> Many of us think that the Treaty should clearly proclaim such
> European values as equality between men and women, non-
> discrimination on grounds of race, religion, sexual orientation, age
> or disability and that it should include express condemnation of
> racism and xenophobia and a procedure for its enforcement.
>
> (Waddington *et al.* 1996, p. 6)

While this may be welcomed as a positive move, it has to be acknowledged that legislation on its own has made only a limited contribution to eliminating racial discrimination (Commission for Racial Equality (CRE) 1992). Of equal importance are strategic policies which have the confidence and active participation of ethnic minorities themselves. Below, I consider the dimension of health which is critical to an understanding of the main topic and illustrative of the scale of social exclusion that ethnic minorities experience.

Good health services are a fundamental necessity to the well-being of all families. An analysis of current research literature from Britain indicates that rates of stillbirth and of perinatal and infant mortality are much higher for some ethnic minority women; low priority is given by service providers to health promotion and prevention; there is meagre availability of translation and interpreting services; ignorance among health professionals about cultural matters such as diet and naming systems is evidenced; the lack of ethnic minority professionals at all levels in the health service is serious and racism is encountered by minorities in their interaction with professionals. This has led one commentator to conclude that:

> The response of the health service has in all but a few cases been
> either to neglect or to marginalize the needs of the Black
> populations. Such has been the state of neglect that Black people
> are seen as a problem.... It is hardly surprising that the responses
> of the health service to date have been characterized by a
> stereotyped view of Black people and their health needs.... The
> need for fundamental change is as pressing as it has ever been.
>
> (Amin and Oppenheim 1992, p. 24)

The same picture can be found in analyses of research on employment, housing and social welfare, and leads to the conclusion that racial inequality is multifaceted in nature and deeply embedded in the kinds of services and possibilities open to ethnic minorities in all aspects of their lives. The damaging impact that this has on ethnic minority disabled persons has received little attention; Redding (1990) has reported how black deaf people have missed out on entitlement and counselling because of lack of monitoring in the deaf community.

Special education from an ethnic minority perspective: what research tells us

Mainstream research can be characterised as largely colour-blind, i.e. it has neglected to acknowledge ethnicity as an integral factor in analysis. Gillborn and Gipps (1996) argue that urgent action is needed in this area: 'If ethnic diversity is ignored...considerable injustices will be sanctioned and enormous potential wasted' (p. 7). This invisibility of ethnicity is more marked in special education research and indicative of failure throughout Europe to debate this issue openly. Current emphasis in the EU is being given to the implementation of the UN Standard Rules (1993) and the Salamanca Statement (UNESCO/ Government of Spain 1994); to date there is no indication that this will explicitly include the rights of disabled people of ethnic minority background.

Published research studies in Britain centre around three key issues which are summarised below.

The question of numbers and placement

The few statistical surveys conducted indicate that there is both over-representation and under-representation in the different categories of disability/learning difficulties and forms of specialised provision. For example, higher numbers of African-Caribbean boys are excluded from school because of behavioural problems, while Asian pupils are highly represented in the categories of severe and profound learning difficulties and sensory impairments and under-represented in the categories of emotional difficulties, language disorders and moderate learning difficulties. Both groups are rarely assessed as dyslexic (Bourne *et al.* 1994, Curnyn *et al.* 1990, Tomlinson 1989).

What is of importance here is that there are inter- and possibly intra-ethnic differences in representation which are reflected in the operation of differing assessment criteria and dynamics. Racial inequality is not even-handed and may surface under different guises: e.g. stereotypes about dysfunctional families or perceived problems associated with heritage languages and cultures (David 1993, Troyna and Siraj-Blatchford 1993). The case for ethnic monitoring couldn't be stronger.

Role and contribution of parents in decision-making

There are just four published studies, which have attempted to research parents' experiences of special education. They report that, despite legislation that was intended to ensure parental rights, families lack information about the whole area of disability/special education, including concepts, terminology, role of professionals, assessment and rights to services. They are seriously under-represented in active decision-making, because of inadequate resources and poor communication between professionals and parents, who are often regarded as passive recipients, particularly Asian women. There have also been reports of discrimination on racial and religious grounds (Blair 1994, Chaudhury 1988, Rehal 1989, Shah 1992).

A number of writers have previously identified general weaknesses in the working of legislation and procedures related to special education, though ethnicity has not featured in their enquiries. Cranwell & Miller (1987), for example, found that one of the major obstacles to active parental involvement in decision-making was the language used by professionals in assessment procedures and written reports: parents were left struggling through pages of confusing jargon, acronyms and labels. Other studies point to the marginalisation of ethnic minority parents by mainstream education and the negative attitudes that teachers may bring to the judgements they make of their pupils' abilities (Tomlinson, 1995; Vincent, 1996). This suggests that those attempting to involve ethnic minority families as genuine partners may face an uphill struggle.

Education policy: curriculum, assessment and support

The quality of the educational experience offered to all pupils is dependent on the match between pupil background and curriculum decisions. The dilemmas inherent in special education and ethnic minorities have been starkly highlighted in an investigation conducted by the CRE (1996). It found evidence of conceptual confusion in professionals' understanding about the relative contribution to learning of first language/English as a second language/bilingualism and learning difficulties. This ambiguity was reflected in the assessment practices which negated the value of pupils' bilingual and bicultural experiences; it also found that the support structures for pupils and families were inadequate.

Perhaps the most disappointing feature of this report is that the academic arguments underpinning bilingualism and learning have long been established. Pioneering work by Cummins (1984) has failed to be translated into action. Professionals still take the view that bilingual pupils with learning difficulties or sensory impairments should be taught in the host language only. Their training has failed to address this issue, and there is also a serious shortage of bilingual, ethnic minority professionals. It is against this background that Diniz and Pal (1997) initiated their study in Scotland.

Ethnic minority parents' perceptions of special education provision (Diniz and Pal 1997)

This qualitative research study is the first of its type in Scotland and was designed to allow parents the opportunity to talk freely about their experiences (Strauss and Corbin 1990). The history of relationships between ethnic minorities and practitioners, including researchers, makes access to families problematic. The families involved are of South Asian origin and were contacted mainly through community networks; their main heritage languages are Hindi, Panjabi, Urdu and Bengali. Both the researchers are of similar background, and one is fluent in three of the languages; an interpreter was needed for Bengali only. Parents were interviewed in the location and language of their choice.

Our analysis of the interviews highlighted four themes which parents spoke about:
- their children's strengths and limitations at home;
- the impact of disability on the family context;
- their experiences of working with professionals;
- their experiences of services, including special education.

In reporting the results here, an attempt is made to offer parents a rare opportunity to be heard, through direct quotation of their views in selected case studies.

Are ethnic minorities all the same?

The study found that having a disabled child has a differential impact on families. Apart from national origin, there is an interplay of factors of cultural heritage, education, language resources (knowledge of English), economic status and family network, which have a significant effect on the family's capacity to respond. I cannot stress too strongly the view gained from the research that stereotyped assumptions about ethnic groups (e.g. that Muslim men will not allow their wives to have their say) can damage access to ethnic minority families, many of whom will have had negative experiences with officialdom.

What is the family's experience of disability and how do they respond?

The overwhelming impression which the families left us with could be characterised as one of isolation and a struggle to be heard. Yet, we were also struck by their fortitude and are in no doubt that they can and did demonstrate positive qualities in responding to adverse circumstances; they were resourceful, supportive of others and showed great perseverance. The mothers in particular felt that white professionals have low expectations of them. The price they pay in terms of time, stress and finance was self-evident.

Case study of Muhammad

The family has lived in Scotland for approximately 18 years; both their children were born here. At the time of the interview, Muhammad, their elder son, was nearly 16 years old. He is severely disabled, attends a special school and is totally dependent on his parents who share in caring for him as they do not have an extended family network nearby. The father sold his business to be at home as his wife's health is deteriorating because of stress; this has brought added financial pressure. Both parents took part in the interview, in which they were distressed; they said they wanted to tell their story to someone. The case illustrates the social and economic sacrifice that the family bears and their feelings of alienation and of being discriminated against. Most of all is their sense of having to struggle to be heard.

Interviewer: So the diet is the problem?

Father: Yes! When we put him on special diet the school authorities didn't agree with that. If we give him the diet which the school advised us to give, then the child gets pain and sometimes feels sick. The mother knows what food is agreeable to his digestive system. But the school does not listen to her views about the diet. The school says that she is too protective. The mother gets worried because the school wants something different from what she wants. It gives her stress. The school doctor says that the child's weight is going down, give him more food. In Hay diet, in the beginning the weight goes down, then after some time it becomes level with normal weight. The school does not take account of the fact that certain food is not agreeable to the child. For eight months it went on but now they accept more and more our system of dieting. They have never cooperated with us. Now his weight is normal. He is healthy. After 12 years if someone is going to the toilet normally then it is a big achievement. Now I do what I think is right for the child, not what they say is right. We have faith in homeopathy. The school thinks that it knows best about our child and [that] we should accept that. They think that we don't know what we are talking about.... If they had been helpful we would have known from the very beginning what we could claim, but we didn't know. We found out from different people at different times. We know now by finding out ourselves, and now we advise other people about the claims....

Lots of people are racially prejudiced. We know some white parents whose children are disabled. From them we found out what various facilities they are getting compared to us. She [mother] did not speak English in the beginning, therefore she did not talk to other white parents, but when her English improved she came to know about discrimination. We have to wait long time to get same facilities. Mostly our people don't know where to complain, and when you complain and they hear an Asian voice they don't take it seriously.... We are worried about the future. What facility will be available for our child in the future? He will be bigger and difficult to handle physically. We are getting older as well. Our strength will not be the same. Then how will we cope? This is the problem. It gives us worry.... We want to take responsibility, but we need support and help.

How responsive are services to ethnic minority families?

The take up of community services is impeded by a lack of knowledge of criteria and mechanisms for accessing entitlement and by a lack of understanding about different professionals' roles, orientations and power relationships. This is especially so in the early years but persists as time passes and needs change. Parents said they needed information about the nature and effects of disability; rarely were they told how home language can foster children's learning. The contribution that qualified and accessible interpreters can make in the early stages of assessment and diagnosis is critical to the welfare of both child and parent; yet, this was not available when needed.

Case study of Rahman

The mother, newly married, arrived in Scotland to join her husband's family who are resident here; a year later she had Rahman. At the time of the interview, Rahman was six and had a brother aged four. He is in Primary 1 in a mainstream school and is undergoing assessment to determine his learning difficulties. His home language is Sylheti (a dialect) and Bengali which he learns at Saturday school. The mother is the main carer as the father works long hours; her knowledge of English is basic. The interview was conducted with the aid of an interpreter. The case highlights the isolation that is experienced and raises questions about early intervention support which is available to the family.

Mother: He has a speech difficulty and problems with eating. When he was six months old, I started giving him solid foods. He started vomiting. I didn't know anything about feeding time or about keeping him on milk or change to solid foods. There was nobody to guide me. I thought that when he is hungry he will cry and that is the only signal for me to give him food.... The health visitor came to the house but I didn't understand what she was saying. I didn't know English and could only say 'Yes' and 'No'. My husband was at work so nobody could interpret for me. My son became weaker.... When he was one year old I took him to hospital. They did many tests on him but they didn't find anything wrong with him. They said that many children have eating problems and he would be OK.

When he was two-and-a-half years old, he had his tonsil operation. During that period his teeth were not growing properly. They seemed rotten and black. I was new to this country. I didn't know what was happening. During that time my in-laws went back to Bangladesh. I couldn't seek help or guidance from anyone....

He went to nursery but much later than other children because I did not know when children start school here. When he was four years old he got a place in nursery. They kept him one extra year because he could not speak properly. He started in primary school when he was six years. He still can't speak properly.... In the nursery the speech therapist used to see him. She told the psychologist. I attended a meeting. The psychologist said when he goes to primary probably he will be OK....

During that period the health visitor came with the interpreter to my house. I said to them, 'Please help me....' The interpreter came only once. You know they can't come very often. This is a government thing. They come when they can, not when you want them. They come through an official channel. For this reason I joined the English class. I went to classes for two years. Without English you can't do anything....

Interviewer: Looking back, where did you get information about what to do?

Mother: I found out myself. I have to go everywhere to get it, from friends, summer school. For this reason I learned English and I also learned to drive. When I think of his childhood, tears come to my eyes [mother wipes eyes]. If I had known how to look after him he wouldn't have been in this situation. I didn't know anything then. I didn't know about life here, I didn't know English and nobody was here to guide me....

How effective is communication with parents?

Parents were particularly critical of the quality of professionals' communication and consultation with them and between professionals. In addition to the complaints of being kept in the dark or side-lined, they reported having to liaise between different parties to ensure that the child's needs were understood by all. A number felt that professionals were too quick to recommend special school placement for their children, which they resisted. How well did parents understand different options available to them?

Case study of Fatima

The family has lived in Scotland for a long time; all seven children were born here. Fatima is the fourth child and one of five daughters. At the time of interview, she was seven and in Primary 2 in a mainstream school; she mainly speaks Panjabi at home and attends Urdu classes on Saturdays. Mother is the main carer as Father works long hours; while she can express herself reasonably in English, she is not literate and relies on her older children for English translation. The case highlights the frustration experienced by the mother in her attempts to get a coordinated response from professionals.

Mother: She is visually impaired ... [Asked when she discovered this.] In P1 [Primary 1]. First the teacher didn't know something was wrong. Teacher said she couldn't concentrate and gets distracted. As time went on, I took her to the hospital. There they told me that she has a problem. I told the headteacher that she needs one-to-one help. The school doctor [psychologist?] said that she should go to special school but I thought she is better where she is.... She is being educated with other children.... She is a lovely child and gets on with everybody... She has a visual problem but otherwise she is normal....

Interviewer: When you look back, what is the first thing you remember?

Mother: I have to run round myself to different agencies to convince them that there is something wrong – the school, hospital, family doctor. I pushed and pushed the matter before them. Had I not pointed again and again strongly, nobody would have noticed something was wrong.... I have spoken to other parents and they say the same thing. They have to do all the running. Only the parents who make a fuss and run around get help. The parents who don't say anything don't get any help. The authorities can't be bothered to help.... More than that, the hospital was not telling the school anything. I have to tell the headteacher. Even the special school doctor who came to the school did not tell the headteacher what was going on.... [Asked why?] I don't know! The headteacher found out only when there was a meeting in the school between the class teacher, headteacher and the special school doctor, and then a 'Record of Needs' was opened. It took so long to establish that. Before this they were not connecting with each other. Now they have a duty to tell each other what is going on.

Are parents active partners in decisions about their children?

There appears to be little common basis upon which decisions about bilingual pupils' special needs can be jointly made with parents. The terminology, legal procedures and dynamics governing special education are a mystery to parents; e.g. rarely did we encounter families who knew what a Record of Needs is. The issue about the potential effects that the child's bicultural and bilingual status has on decisions about possible learning difficulties needs to be explicitly acknowledged. We have cases in which it is far from clear whether problems cited as evidence of learning difficulties arise from genuine individual limitations of a child's capacities or are a consequence of the school's failure to recognise and cater for bilingual and bicultural needs.

How does racial inequality feature in the experience of parents?

Parents were reluctant to talk about racism, but they were clear in their views about the less favourable treatment which they perceived they were receiving. There is a strong feeling that negative attitudes and stereotyping leads to minority families receiving inequitable services (*see* 'Case study of Muhammad' p.113). Another family voiced the matter as follows:

> How can there be proper consultation when the authorities think that we Asians don't have the same understanding and knowledge as them and cannot express our ideas properly? They think that we cannot challenge them. Therefore they ignore our views and impose their own.

Conclusions: what are the implications for policy and practice?

This chapter set out to consider the interaction between ethnic minority families and services for children with SEN. It might be assumed that community services are designed to cater for all sectors of a diverse society. The findings of the Scottish study, supported by analyses of the available literature, appear to raise serious doubts about the validity of such claims and signal the extent to which matters will have to change in order that ethnic minorities are equitably provided for. All the parents we have encountered in our study wanted to and needed to be active partners in providing for their children. At an individual level, the majority of professionals would also subscribe to this objective. So, what measures might be instituted to combat barriers and secure much needed improvement? Listed below are priorities for policy and practice; Shah (1992) has also offered very valuable practical strategies for professionals working with Asian families of disabled children.

Priorities for policy

The case for monitoring service provision to different ethnic groups is a quality matter; it is about improving standards for all. This is unlikely to be achieved until policy-related research and statistics provide analyses by ethnic classification as a matter of course. Such a race-explicit, rather than colour-blind, approach would signal a commitment to tackle some of the issues of racial inequality pinpointed above. Families must be active partners in this exercise and be convinced that the results will be put to effective use. If ethnic diversity is ignored, enormous damage will continue to be inflicted on ethnic minorities and society as a whole (Gillborn and Gipps 1996).

It is evident that the planning of services should be undertaken on a more holistic, inter-agency basis if the multifaceted barriers which ethnic minorities face are to be tackled; division of responsibilities by departments creates boundaries which do not often serve families' interests. The issue of language(s) and cultural differences is an important component if families are to participate actively in statutory decision-making procedures; in particular, trained interpretation and translation personnel are a necessity.

Recruitment of bilingual and bicultural professionals remains a priority. Universities have an important role to play in increasing opportunities for ethnic minorities to qualify in the range of careers. Meanwhile, staff development at all levels should be provided; training should concentrate less on issues and more on practical strategies for improving and monitoring effective partnership with ethnic minority families. Involving the latter in training initiatives is likely to make them more fruitful, learning with, rather than about them!

Tomlinson's (1995) argument for a new statutory framework for schools to create home–school associations by which all parents, including those from ethnic minorities, are given a voice in the decision-making process is a compelling one.

Priorities for practitioners

'Partnership with parents', so often proclaimed as a cornerstone of special education is far from the reality experienced by ethnic minorities. An honest acknowledgement of the reality of professional power and racial inequality as systemic forces is the first step to taking positive action. Too often one hears the view, 'Not me; I'm not prejudiced', rather than, 'How do our school procedures, processes and ethos promote active involvement, and how do we know?' The route to change is through whole-school commitment and leadership; current models developed for mainstream partnership should be extended to include ethnic minority parents (Hornby 1995).

There is a substantial literature on theory and practice of bilingualism and learning, cultural diversity and curriculum, ethnicity and social policy (Bourne and McPake 1991, Hall 1995, Ranger *et al.* 1996, Siraj-Blatchford 1994, Skutnabb-Kangas and Cummins 1997, Troyna 1993). This should form the basis for school-based staff development for all staff and parents.

Professionals should get to know communities; be aware of ethnic differences but have high expectations of all parents; visit them; make demands on Interpreting and English as a Second Language services; and work with professionals across boundaries.

I conclude with a thought worth repeating. Ethnic diversity is not solely an inner-city issue nor confined to a few states in the EU. Recent estimates suggest that there are 12–15 million non-citizen residents alone (Eurostats 1996). They are here to stay and have legitimate rights and aspirations. Are disabled children of ethnic minority background receiving an education appropriate to their cultural backgrounds? The response appears to be, 'We don't know. It is not yet an issue!' Whereas the chapter has concentrated on the situation within Britain, the issues raised are thus of equal significance to all European states. It appears that findings of the OECD (1987) report, referred to in the introduction, have yet to be addressed.

Chapter 10

Early intervention services to children with special needs: a Welsh study

Elizabeth Jones and Jean Ware

Introduction

This chapter describes an ongoing study of early intervention services for children with special needs in the former county of South Glamorgan (approximately the area covered since 1996 by the two unitary authorities of Cardiff and the Vale of Glamorgan and Barry). The study aims to discover the range of provision available to different children and their families, and the factors which influence the services they receive. In particular it focuses on the organisation of services and the way in which families experience the provision of services from birth to age six. We are particularly interested in how the actual experiences of families fit with theoretical perspectives on 'good provision'.

Background

South Glamorgan has had early intervention services for children with special needs for 20 years, having been the setting for one of the two pilot schemes for the Portage service when this was first introduced into the UK in 1976 (Clements *et al.* 1980, Revill and Blunden 1979). The original pilot scheme was run over a six-month period and the initial results were regarded as very positive, with the children who participated in the pilot scheme making significant gains in terms both of the number skills learned during the course of the project and of increased scores on the Griffiths Mental Development Scale (Revill and Blunden 1979, Wilcock 1981). As a result of the pilot schemes the service had been extended to the whole of South Glamorgan by 1981 (Dunn 1992, personal communication) and a

National Portage Service was set up in the UK (Kushlick 1984, cited in Sturmey and Crisp 1986).

In the intervening years, as in other parts of the UK, a number of other services for young children with special needs have emerged, funded and run by a range of statutory and voluntary organisations (including the All Wales Strategy, a government-funded scheme unique to Wales (Welsh Office 1994). Thus the Home Advisory Service is now one of many services in the area for children under five with special needs. However, when we commenced our study, there appeared to be no overall directory or comprehensive list of services for young children with special needs in South Glamorgan.

We felt therefore that a study of provision in South Glamorgan was likely to be particularly revealing in terms of how provision had developed since the initial introduction of the Portage pilot scheme. Additionally one of us had already developed good links with some of the service providers involved through an earlier small study (Jones 1994), thus access was unlikely to prove problematic.

The study

The study was divided into two main parts:
- a survey of provision which was intended to map the services available in South Glamorgan;
- in-depth interviews with parents aimed at uncovering their experiences and perceptions of the service they had received.

By using this two-pronged approach, we hoped to address the issues of: how different factors (such as location within the region, the severity and type of the child's disability) affected service provision; the accessibility to parents of information about services and the amount of choice available to them; and the extent to which the provision actually experienced by families fitted with current thinking on good practice. This chapter is mainly concerned with the first part of the study.

Fit with current theoretical perspectives

Within the research literature, there has been a move away from a within-child model of disability over the past 100 years towards a more family-focused model (Carpenter this volume, Dixon and Flanagan

1984, Ferri and Saunders 1991, Guralnick 1991). We were therefore interested in service providers' perceptions of their own focus on the child as an individual with a disability or more widely on the needs of the family as a whole.

Accessibility of information to parents

A number of authors suggest that access to accurate and comprehensive information relating to service provision is an important prerequisite to supplying a high-quality service to children with SEN and their families. The discovery, therefore, that there was no comprehensive directory of services in South Glamorgan suggested that it was particularly important to examine the quality of information available to parents and professionals in the area.

Impact of child's disability on choice and availability of services

Anecdotal evidence from some service providers suggested that severity of disability was a particular factor in the amount of choice available to parents. We therefore wished to identify the extent to which a choice was available to parents and whether specific factors had influenced this choice.

Conducting the research

Phase 1: a survey of provision

The diversity and apparently *ad hoc* nature of services in South Glamorgan indicated by the lack of a comprehensive register meant that it was not easy to select a study sample. We therefore decided to carry out a total census of services using a snowballing technique (Oppenheim 1992). Data was collected through a series of structured interviews using the interview guide as outlined by Patton (1983). Ideas for appropriate questions were taken from Ferri and Saunders (1991) and questions were designed to identify:
- the main focus of the intervention;
- what was involved for the child and the family;

- who was responsible for referring children;
- specific criteria used by organisations for placing children with SEN into particular services;
- the catchment area for inclusion;
- the factors that influenced the type of intervention a child might receive.

Phase 2: parents' experience of services

This phase of the research involved the interviewing of parents of six-year-old children in South Glamorgan who have a statement of SEN or who were undergoing assessment for a statement. The interviews were geared towards exploring parental accounts of their own and their child's experiences of service provision, in particular:

- parents' experiences of diagnosis of their child's disability;
- the process of referral to intervention services;
- the types and amount of service received;
- the amount of choice they were able to exercise in selecting a service for their child;
- factors which influenced parental choice of service for their children;
- parents' perceptions of their involvement with professionals in deciding upon provision for their child.

Results of Phase 1

In all 50 interviews were conducted with service representatives who were potential providers of early intervention services. Of these, 40 proved to be direct suppliers of early intervention services to children with SEN. Thus the results of Phase 1 are based on content analysis of these 40 interviews.

Services available in South Glamorgan

The analysis showed that the types of early intervention available in South Glamorgan could be grouped in two ways:

- according to the focus and methods of the intervention;
- according to the agency/ies responsible for funding and supplying the intervention.

Who was the service aimed at and how was it delivered?
Examination of answers relating to what was involved in implementing the intervention revealed that the foci of interventions in South Glamorgan were educational, social, health and ecological. Services were administered in individual- and group-based settings and in a combination of the two.

The flow chart (Figure 10.1) shows the categorisation of services according to focus and method of delivery. Educational and social interventions included both individual- and group-based provision while all therapy provision was individually delivered. Perhaps, not surprisingly, ecological interventions featured combined group and individual provision.

The way in which the services could be grouped according to focus and method of delivery closely reflected the findings of Shonkoff *et al.* (1992). Shonkoff *et al.* investigated service location and found services were either home-based, centre-based or mixed. Furthermore, they found that service format could be individual, group or mixed. However, any attempt at analysis inevitably simplifies the complexity of provision; for example, schools and nurseries were involved in the delivery of social and therapy intervention as well as group-based and individual-based teaching.

Educational
Individual educational provision included skills-based teaching provided by the Home Advisory Service, peripatetic teaching for visually and hearing impaired children provided by the LEA and by the Royal National Institute for the Blind (RNIB), and a School for Parents provided by Scope.

Special schools, integrated nursery schools, units and classes attached to mainstream schools and the Children's Intensive Support Service provided both group-based and IEPs.

Social
Group-based social intervention services were provided by playgroups, social services Family Centres and nurseries. Individual social intervention was supplied through Chwarae Arbennig Gartref (Special Play at Home Scheme) and, if appropriate to the family's needs, social services' 'Care to Share' Scheme. In addition, group-based activities in school and nursery also provided opportunities for social intervention.

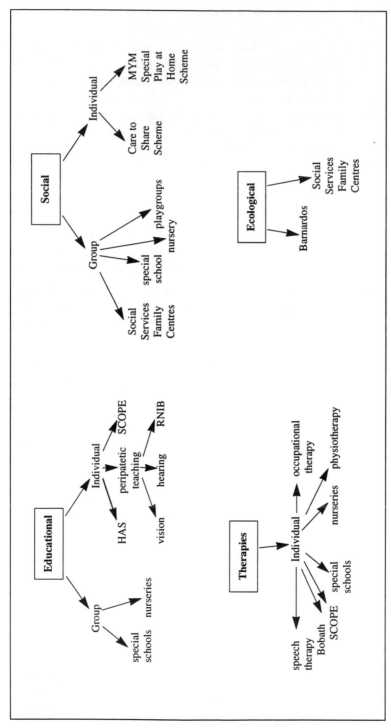

Figure 10.1 Types of early intervention services in South Glamorgan according to focus and method of delivery

Therapies

Therapy services included physiotherapy, occupational therapy and speech therapy, all under the auspices of the health service, Bobath Cymru and Scope's School for Parents. In addition, some schools were also responsible for the implementation of therapies, such as speech and physiotherapy, during the school day.

Ecological

The interview data revealed the provision of two types of ecological intervention: one provided by Barnardo's and the other by social services. The intervention supplied by Barnardo's was multi-dimensional in the sense that it appeared to cater for all aspects of child and family need. Services included social interaction from the playgroup, group and individual teaching at the Centre, individual teaching at home (if required), skill-based teaching with self-defined goals and developmental assessment, toy loaning, an advice service from parents regarding other services in the area, benefit entitlement, etc. and a secondhand clothes shop. The intervention supplied by social services also appeared to cater for all aspects of child and family need. Services included day-care and nursery provision, a baby-sitting service when appropriate, advice and guidance on subjects ranging from healthy eating, contraception and 'well woman' issues to claiming social security benefits, equipment (e.g. baths and prams) available for loan, short-term respite provision, a drop-in centre and monthly visits from a link worker to families of children attending the Centre.

Who pays for early intervention in South Glamorgan?

The interview questionnaire had contained questions directly related to funding and running of intervention services. Analysis of the answers revealed funding of services was a complex process; however, the main agencies found to be responsible for funding and operating early intervention in South Glamorgan were health, education, social services, charities and the All Wales Strategy. All these agencies have funded interventions both individually and jointly.

Services funded by one agency in South Glamorgan

The LEA funded a peripatetic teaching service for children with hearing and visual impairments (*see* Figure 10.2), six special schools with places for children under five, three mainstream schools with attached nursery units offering integrated provision to children with special needs, two mainstream schools with special needs units

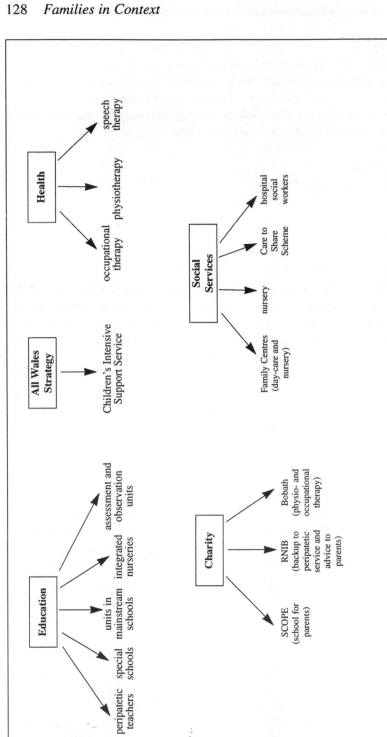

Figure 10.2 Single agency funded early intervention services in South Glamorgan

attached catering for the 'rising fives', two integrated nurseries, a mainstream primary school which offered a nursery and a special needs observation and assessment unit which included two special needs classrooms.

The RNIB funds the provision of advice to families of children with a visual disability and also a back-up service to the Vision peripatetic teaching service funded by the LEA, especially to families who have children under two with visual impairment because the education service has no legal obligation to provide services for such children.

The health authority is responsible for providing and funding therapies. This includes physio-, occupational and speech therapy. The voluntary sector also funds and provides therapy. For example, occupational and physiotherapy form part of the service provided through Bobath Cymru and Scope.

Three Family Centres providing day-care and nursery places for children, whose ages range from eight weeks to four years, were funded by social services. They were also responsible for funding and providing two hospital social workers in the region, an integrated day nursery based in a small rural town, and a 'Care to Share' Scheme. This scheme supplied a number of services to families of children with physical disabilities where there was felt to be a deficit in service provision in the region. Services provided depended upon the individual family's needs, and ranged from one-to-one stimulation of the child to general respite care.

Services provided by more than one agency
Barnardo's provide a multidimensional service from a base in a Family Centre which is jointly funded by Barnardo's themselves and social services (*see* Figure 10.3). The services provided include a playgroup, individual teaching at the Centre, individual teaching at home, developmental assessments, toy loaning and advice service, advice to parents regarding services and benefits, and a secondhand clothing shop.

An integrated playgroup service is funded by social services and the Education Department, but provided by National Children's Homes Cymru. Social services and the Church of England jointly fund a Family Centre which provides day-care and nursery facilities in the Vale of Glamorgan. Integrated playgroup provision is also provided in the medium of Welsh and English through the Pre-school Playgroups Association, the Under-fives Scheme and Mudiad Ysgolion Meithrin. The playgroups are funded by social services and the All Wales Strategy,

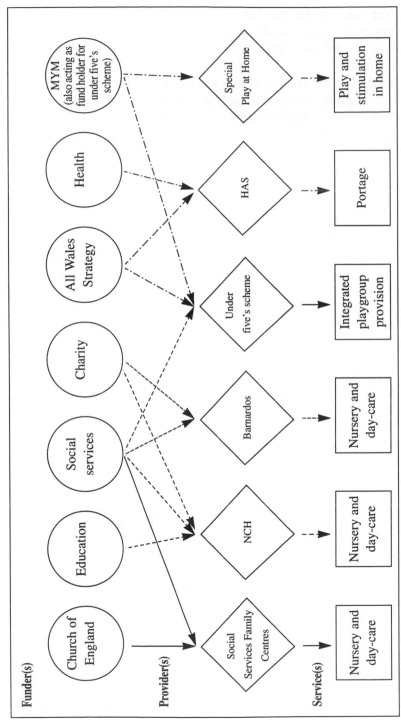

Figure 10.3 Joint agency funded early intervention services in South Glamorgan

the host agency for funding being Mudiad Ysgolion Meithrin. The playgroups are jointly organised and run by a management committee which is hosted by the Under-fives Scheme. Mudiad Ysgolion Meithrin also funds independently a small-scale Chwarae Arbennig Gartref (Special Play at Home Scheme) for very disabled and sick children. The South Glamorgan Home Advisory Service is jointly funded through the local area health authority and the All Wales Strategy.

Finally, parents are expected to make a financial contribution to some of the early intervention programmes available in South Glamorgan, such as the Under-fives Scheme, depending upon their economic means.

Limitation of choice of service

Types of intervention children receive according to their difficulties

Preliminary analysis of the data collected in the first phase of the research suggested that there was a link between the number of services available to a child and the severity of the child's disability; that is, that there were fewer services available to children with more severe and profound disabilities than those with mild to moderate disabilities. The interviews with service providers suggested that children with mild to moderate difficulties received a higher number of services before progressing into the education sector because children with severe and profound learning difficulties were referred by professionals to commence their school career as young as age two. Therefore, receipt of educational provision at this age disqualified many children with severe and profound learning difficulties from receiving any of the other types of service available. Furthermore, some of the service providers interviewed indicated that although they tried to serve all children equally regardless of degree of disability, other factors such as fire regulations applying to the building in which the intervention service was provided prevented the service being granted to those with the more severe physical disabilities. In addition, other service providers indicated that although they claimed to serve all children equally regardless of level of physical disability or learning difficulty, the majority of their clients fell within the mild to severe level of disability.

At first the data collection for the second phase of the research (with the parents of children aged six who were resident in South Glamorgan and had a statement of SEN) appeared to support this hypothesis. However, when this phase had been completed and analysed, we found that the amount of service provision referrals children received was not connected to the level of disability or difficulty experienced by the child, but to whether or not children had been referred to or through the Children's Centre connected to two of the hospitals in the county. We believe this to be a particularly significant finding which has important implications for service providers in the area, and one of us (Jones, forthcoming) is currently carrying out further investigations in order to discover what factors determine referral to the Children's Centres.

Equality of service provision for Welsh and English speakers

There were a number of services which offered Welsh medium provision to children under five with SEN in South Glamorgan; for example, a Play at Home Scheme, integrated playgroup provision and a speech therapy service. Nevertheless, despite the discovery of these services it must be noted that some were small, low key services which were therefore limited in terms of amount of service provision they were able to offer. For example, despite the discovery of the existence of a speech therapy service available in the medium of Welsh, the service was, by admission, informal and provided only one morning of therapy per week.

With regard to overall availability of provision in the medium of Welsh some service providers indicated that there was a limitation of choice of special schools for Welsh-speaking children with SEN who had received pre-school provision in the medium of Welsh. We found this limitation of choice of service to be particularly apparent for children with severe or profound learning difficulties, who faced a choice from a number of special schools, all of which were English medium. Similarly, there was less choice found to be available to children who had a specific speech or language difficulty but not a learning difficulty. (There is only one school in the area which caters for children with such difficulties – and this is an English medium school.) Many of the service providers interviewed highlighted that they were unable to provide services in the medium of Welsh to parents who expressed a desire for their children to receive services in Welsh language because of a number of constraints. Chief among these were:
- the need to prioritise and use limited budgets and funding to cater for the majority rather than the minority;
- the lack of trained fluent Welsh speakers in the appropriate service.

In order to justify the inability to fund and provide the same choice of service in the medium of Welsh which would cater for the minority of Welsh speakers in the population at the expense of providing adequate services to the majority of English speakers in the population, one service provider stated: 'Most people can speak English. If we do a visit to a child who is Welsh we can communicate with the parent and use the parent as an interpreter.'

The choice was found not to be as limited for those children with general mild to moderate learning difficulties, who were able to opt for a Welsh language education in integrated provision or in units at one of the Welsh language schools in the area. In our view this question merits further investigation.

The rural/urban divide and the effect of boundary changes

Many of the service providers interviewed during the period 1994–5 stressed concerns that the proposed Welsh Office boundary changes which were implemented on 1 April 1996 would adversely affect the children's access and entitlement to a variety of choice of service provided. Preliminary analysis of the parental interviews conducted since the implementation of the boundary changes indicate that these fears have been realised. Parents indicated that some services offer specialist provision for children with specific or low incidence disabilities which are only available from within the urban region of the area. However, since the changes of April 1996, those living in the rural area have found their access to these speciality services situated in the urban area limited because they are now residing in an area governed by a different authority to the one that is providing the service needed by their child. This view was supported by local headteachers at a recent conference held by Awdurdod Cwricwlwm ac Asesu Cymru (ACAC)/SCAA.

Parents also indicated that they felt that there was an urban/rural divide with regard to access to and choice of services. Parents living in the rural area of the county have indicated that the geographic isolation of the area limits the choice of available services.

Problems in obtaining accurate and up-to-date information

Vagueness of the term 'need'

In carrying out the study we experienced great difficulty in finding out which services provided what interventions to whom, and who the key person was to contact in order to obtain information about provision. This problem particularly applied to provision of integrated nurseries by social services Family Centres in the area. It took three months of letters and telephone calls to ascertain which Family Centres provided services to children with SEN and to arrange interviews with the person in charge of each Family Centre. It proved problematic to ascertain who supplied provision to children with special needs because of the ambiguity of the term, 'need', in legislation. Campion (1992) highlights the confusion which occurs between children considered to have SEN because of social problems, and those who have SEN because of learning or physical difficulties. Mittler (Visser and Upton 1993) notes that the Children Act which came into force in October 1991 is probably the most important piece of legislation about children on the statute book because it mandates joint action to identify and meet the needs of all children who require additional provision by the local authority as a whole, not just the LEA. However, he criticises those who drafted the Children Act for not learning from the limitations of the 1981 Education Act because needs have not clearly been defined and resources have not been made available to implement the Act properly.

Lack of available documentation regarding service provision

Brewer and Kakalik (1979), in their two-year cross-agency evaluation in the USA, identified insufficient information as one of the major factors which resulted in the disorganisation, complexity and fragmentation of the health, education and welfare services. Many of the service providers interviewed noted that there was no documentation available to inform them of total availability of early intervention services in South Glamorgan. Service providers were expected to collate details of available services through their experience in the job; this particularly applied to medical social workers and special needs health visitors whose role involved advising parents of available services, and acting as advocates for parents with other professionals providing intervention. They noted it was particularly difficult to keep abreast of new services being created or old ones ceasing to exist or changing name. This proved to be particularly problematic for low key services with small budgets.

These findings have implications for networking practice as found by Carpenter and Herbert (1994c) who note: 'Professionals need to know the network within their area in order that they can make it available to parents who should not be expected to undertake this search alone' (p. 56).

Preliminary analysis of the interviews with parents also indicate their frustration because of a lack of documentary information available.

What do service providers consider constitutes a family unit?

Analysis of the service provider interview transcripts revealed that 34 of the 40 service providers interviewed regarded the main focus of the intervention to be both the child and the child's family. The move towards family-focused intervention and the involvement of the child's parents is indicative of the increased realisation by professionals of the importance of parental involvement with service providers which is upheld by the 1994 Code of Practice.

However, it is interesting to note that service providers appear to view the family as consisting of mother (or primary care-giver) and child. Of the 40 service providers interviewed, only one service provider noted the importance of including and helping the father, as well as the mother and the child, with the intervention. Similar results were found by Carpenter and Herbert (1994c), who noted in their study problems of access to professionals for fathers of children with SEN. They gave one possible explanation that the majority of support services work only during the day when many fathers are at work. In the interview, the service provider noted how they attempt to overcome the problem of lack of access to fathers due to working hours with a number of strategies. She stated:

> What I have tried to do in the past, but it's not always possible in theory ... but one of the things I worry about is the dads. I rarely meet the dads, though one or two dads.... There is one up the road, and out of four visits I have seen him once, and I try to organise my visits to fit in with his shifts. A way of overcoming it ... I used to try to leave something with the parents, just a sheet of paper so they could talk about it. And then I would try and copy bits of video that we had of their child, try and put it on a video so that the parents could look at it together and try and discuss together at a later time.

She also noted the importance of the role of both parents: 'Both parents have a role, don't they, in fostering their child's development, and they are both equally upset after diagnosis, so it has got to be both.'

This in turn should have important implications for providers of services to adapt and make services more flexible to include both parents.

Conclusion

The preliminary analysis has yielded both positive and negative results relating to the provision of services to children with SEN in the South Glamorgan area. The number and variety of services discovered to be in operation in the county are a positive factor in meeting the needs of children with SEN and their families. In particular, the existence of special low key services which attempted to address specific and otherwise uncatered for difficulties was especially encouraging. However, effective utilisation of these numerous services was hampered by the lack of easily accessible and up-to-date information for both parents and professionals. Parent and professional awareness of service provision could be heightened if an accurate list of services provided in the area was compiled which could then be updated on a regular basis. However, this study also identified a number of factors which could potentially have a negative impact on the provision of appropriate and effective early intervention services in South Glamorgan. The most salient of these factors were:

- the role of the children's centre as a 'gatekeeper' of services;
- the narrow concept of the family as being the child and main caregiver apparently held by some service providers;
- the lack of provision through the medium of Welsh;
- the implications of local government reorganisation resulting in the formation of smaller unitary authorities;
- the lack of choice of service available to those living in more rural areas within the county.

It should be noted that this last factor has emerged in other studies in Wales – for example, in parental choice of secondary school (Reynolds 1995) – and may well be an issue in other relatively thinly populated areas. Similarly, the issue of the lack of Welsh medium provision for pupils with SEN is anecdotally reported across all phases of schooling.

Further, detailed investigation of the impact of these factors could inform service provision not only in this area of South Wales but more widely in the UK and elsewhere.

Part IV: Initiatives in research and practice

Chapter 11

Curriculum issues in early childhood: implications for families

Tricia David, Jenny Moir and Elaine Herbert

Families: at the heart of the education process

Caitlin (seven months) sits on her mother's lap and 'plays the piano', while her grandparents sit in rapt attention. She stops occasionally to receive their applause. By nine months she is deliberately moving her position so as to alter the range of notes accessible to her tiny reach but she is still pausing for the admiration.

* * * * *

Imran (nine months) clutches the television remote control gadget with a satisfied glow. As with some of the other objects in his daily life, he has already comprehended which hold a key to power over aspects of the family's life.

There is a scene in the film *Peter's Friends* when Peter points out how each of us comes into a family as if we have been dropped, randomly, down a chimney and that thereafter we have to make the best of things. According to recent research (Trevarthen 1992), babies and young children are 'programmed' to make sense of the context in which they 'find themselves'. They do indeed try to 'make the best of things'.

However, while some children become part of a family where their understandings are nurtured, where they, together with other family members, gradually increase their understandings of 'the world' and co-construct the meanings of the lives they share together, others struggle to do so. The reasons some of our young children find their attempts at 'making sense' more of a struggle than others are numerous.

They may have been born into a family where there are high levels of stress, through poverty and other factors, or where parental disadvantage and lack of knowledge, or demands on adult time and attention, leave little for the new family member. The child's own learning difficulties may mean some parents need to further develop their own skills in order to communicate effectively with their child. In addition, some families may not receive sufficient support from 'outside' – whether that be from their own extended family or from workers in the field in the UK. Young families, or perhaps more accurately young mothers, do seem to be expected to cope in relative isolation in this country. Although the Rowntree Foundation report (Utting 1995) recognises the help which extended families offer, often despite geographical constraints, its author also remarks on the discrepancy between national rhetoric on the importance of the family in the upbringing of children compared with the paucity of investment in support services.

Parents and early childhood education provision

Twenty years ago only one in four mothers of children under five was in paid employment, whereas by 1992 the proportion had risen to just under 50 per cent. Meanwhile, government policy even today reflects the view that parenting, and thus child care, is a private matter (DfEE 1996a). The issue then is the lack of edu-care services for children under five.

Day-care services in which education is embedded are in short supply in the UK, especially for children under two.[1] This is the result of long-term neglect on the part of successive governments. It also indicates ignorance of the damage we may be inflicting on children's attitudes to learning by treating them as parcels rather than people.

The high levels of staffing required in order to provide stimulation and interaction, the need for staff to be well-trained and well-paid, means that such provision is financially costly. For research has shown that dissatisfied staff move on regularly and do not form the positive, meaningful relationships children need at this stage, nor can parents and staff form supportive partnerships (Whitebrook *et al.* 1990). However, a long-term calculation might convince us that *not* investing during a child's early years costs society more in the long run, as the High/Scope research from the USA has demonstrated (Schweinhart and Weikart 1993).

Various studies have indicated that babies and very young children can benefit from group provision as long as attention has been paid to their individuality, their need for adult familiarity and responsiveness, and for interaction with other children (Goldschmeid and Jackson 1994, Goldschmeid and Selleck 1996): aspects the majority of us would probably define as indicators of high quality, despite the debate about the value-laden nature of judgements of quality.

Constructions of childhood and cultural expectations

Until relatively recently the context-bound nature of childhood had not been fully recognised. Since the 1979 publication of William Kessen's 'The American child and other cultural inventions' (Bronfenbrenner 1979), we have become more aware of the ways in which different societies impose different childhoods, with different expectations, on the young.

In Denmark or Brazil it would be unthinkable to assess four year olds on their reading achievements, yet here in the UK there is the expectation that by the time they enter reception class, which is often before they are five, British children will be able to recognise letters, words and numerals (SCAA 1996).

What do we mean by 'curriculum' for young children?

Wherever children are, they will be learning, and a curriculum of some sort will be operating, even if the adults are unaware of this fact. The curriculum is the totality of learning opportunities, which offer the skills, knowledge, concepts and attitudes children can acquire through experience with their peers, 'knowledgeable others' and the environment.

In most of the member countries of the EU, the curriculum for children below primary school age is thought of in terms of areas of experience and is made accessible to the children through play. With the advent of the National Curriculum in the UK for children aged 5 to 16, together with parental demand for improved access to nursery education, the government created a scheme intended to encourage voluntary and private nursery providers to increase the number of places available for four-year-olds (*see* DfEE 1996b).

While many early years practitioners had already seen the 'areas of experience' model of the curriculum suggested in the Rumbold Report

(Department of Education and Science (DES) 1990) as a meaningful way forward, in 1996 the UK Secretary of State for Education and Employment, Gillian Shephard, set SCAA the task of drawing up new curriculum guidelines. These were finally published as *Desirable Outcomes for Children's Learning* (SCAA 1996), and they are linked to a proposed baseline assessment scheme for children entering their first class of primary school. Such assessments are expected to fulfil two purposes: first, to diagnose learning needs, and, second, to provide a score which will be compared with the scores children achieve at the end of KS 1 (aged almost seven), such that a school's 'value-added' measure can be calculated.

Although it is claimed that SCAA's 'desirable outcomes' (SCAA 1996) are not a curriculum, it is impossible to imagine that its areas of learning, and the emphasis on literacy and numeracy in various statements from SCAA, OFSTED and the DfEE, will not result in a curriculum intended to 'prepare children' for the National Curriculum. It may be left to the registered nursery inspectors, recently trained and appointed to monitor the implementation of the SCAA proposals, to ensure that play remains the most appropriate vehicle for both children's learning and observation-based assessments. The top-down pressure on teachers of four-year-olds could otherwise lead to an overly formal approach, which in turn would impact on the lives and learning of children under four. Research has shown (Shorrocks 1992) that children who, during their pre-school years, experienced a traditional nursery 'play-oriented' curriculum, in which most activities were child-directed, outperformed their peers in the KS 1 tasks and tests for seven-year-olds.

Each of us carries around a notion of our cultural group's expectations of children (and adults) at different stages in their lives. That these expectations impinge more negatively on children whose progress, for a host of reasons, may be noticeably slower than others in certain areas, is an issue both educators and parents must address. But each child is unique, both biologically and ecologically, and each family is unique, requiring that those of us working in the field not only make our meanings about early learning clear, but that we enter into the shared meanings and understanding of the world that children and their parents have already developed together.

Curriculum development within the inclusive nursery

As the child becomes ready to enter the more formal setting of the nursery, new relationships must be established.

Early years teachers readily acknowledge the notion of 'parents as partners' or 'parents as first educators' (DES 1978). However, familiarity should not lend complacency to this very real challenge, and the early years practitioner needs to develop responsive and effective ways of realising this ideal for *all* children, but perhaps most especially for those children with special learning needs.

Since the balance of information at this time is within the gift of the family, it is essential that the pre-school teacher offers to visit the family in their own home where their ownership of knowledge and expertise can be acknowledged. Home visits are not primarily opportunities for teachers to parade their knowledge and expertise, but rather an opportunity for them to listen, observe and ask questions, so that they can begin to appreciate the unique context for learning that each child brings with them to their classroom, and to assess how to build bridges to enable each child to make sense of the learning environment they are about to encounter.

Families need to be able to see that home visits are an opportunity to tell early years practitioners about their children: their talents, their difficulties and their social and emotional needs. They should not feel that any kind of judgement is being made about their style of child-rearing, home-making or family relationships. Given this approach, it is one nursery's experience that approximately 95 per cent of families accept the offer of a home visit each year prior to their school attendance, and that, within this group, 100 per cent of families with children with an SEN have accepted a home visit prior to school attendance. As a result of these visits, a profile of each child's development is compiled by the parents or carers, with as little or as much help as is needed from nursery staff. These profiles prove an invaluable aid when devising appropriate learning opportunities for all children and are especially helpful in devising IEPs for those children with SEN (DfE 1994).

These following examples of transitional programmes were set up in response to the needs and requests of the families concerned. None has been replicated, for it is for the school to be responsive to the unique needs of each family and to enable each family to ask for what they need for their 'special' children (Herbert and Moir 1996).

Katie, a hearing child with a severe language disorder, was able to communicate only through signs from the Makaton vocabulary (Walker 1985). Katie's mother asked if she and her daughter could visit nursery on a number of occasions, prior to her attendance at nursery, in order to take photographs of Katie playing in the various play areas. She incorporated these into a story-scrapbook about 'Going to nursery' so that Katie could familiarise herself with the nursery at home, with her family, using the new nursery-based Makaton vocabulary agreed upon by her mother and the nursery teacher.

* * * * *

Jaswinder, who had never separated from his parents and who had spent many weeks and months of his first two years in hospital, was developmentally delayed. On numerous occasions in the term preceding his starting in the nursery, he would walk to the nursery gate with his father and his now familiar pre-school teacher. Initially, he would wave goodbye to his father and walk round the school gardens; after a while he entered the nursery with his pre-school teacher for a brief play before returning to his father at the school gate. When the time came to say goodbye to his father and join his peers in the nursery in the care of the nursery teacher, he was able to do so with confidence and with a sense of security.

A partnership between home and school, built on such firm foundations, will lead to further opportunities to work cooperatively in the best interests of the child. The families of children with an SEN often require more time for discussion with the class teacher (Carpenter and Herbert 1994b).

Answering the needs of all children in an inclusive nursery

Primarily a nursery which welcomes children with SEN is one where credence is given to the notion that each child is unique and has individual needs. The additional teaching skills that develop from working alongside specialist agencies such as speech therapists, physiotherapists and pre-school teachers can be utilised when working with *all* children in the nursery. Such teachers and classroom assistants become more skilled at task analysis, at using differentiated modes of questioning, and they become better able to use daily observations to support and 'scaffold' children's learning (Vygotsky 1978). Children too have additional learning opportunities when they are able to share their environment with children whose needs are clearly different from their own in many respects.

Julie used a rollator to move around the nursery. Her peers learned to think of the other person and anticipate Julie's needs. They would hand her a paper towel realising that to use a rollator with wet hands was both difficult and potentially dangerous. They also discovered that she was an excellent bouncer and 'giggler' in the soft play area.

* * * * *

Michael's need fell within the autistic spectrum. He found it very difficult to sit still at story time and would tend to disturb the other children unless they allowed him quietly to trace the raised patterns on the soles of their shoes over and over again. The children soon learned to accept and understand that Michael had needs and behaviours which they had to accommodate because he was a 'special' member of the group.

Becoming a part signing environment (e.g. Makaton) for hearing impaired or language disordered or delayed children, has enriched the language environment of the nursery for all children, giving them the opportunity to learn the rudiments of another language or form of communication. Similarly, as part of the early reading experience, interpretation of symbols is a standard part of the nursery curriculum.

Symbols from a standardised augmentative communication system (Detheridge and Detheridge 1997) are used to label play areas (alongside large scripted signs) and to make planning cards for the children (Schweinhart and Weikart 1993). The nursery is divided into 12 distinct play areas which reflect a breadth of play experiences covering the full range of early years curriculum areas. At the beginning of each session, children are given the opportunity to plan their own activities, and the plan is stored in a clear, plastic wallet. Each child can return to their plan to 'read' it without needing adult support. The children are expected to manage these plans with an increasing degree of independence and responsibility as the nursery year progresses.

All the children use this system, and those with an SEN have been able to access this type of responsible, self-initiated planning, providing some adult support has been given during the play session. Thus these symbols readily enable children to understand the notion that a written symbol can carry meaning.

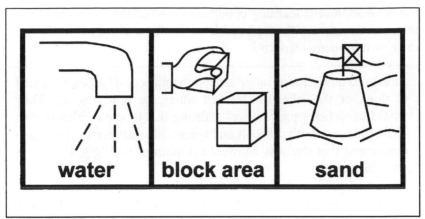

Figure 11.1   Play labels

There are unpredictable advantages of offering all children such a 'special', yet inclusive, curriculum (Carpenter 1995c). The experience of Muneeza and her family illustrates this.

Muneeza's SEN had remained unidentified prior to her nursery attendance. Within the first few days of nursery, parental concerns about slow speech development were soon identified as a significant difficulty with both receptive and expressive language development. While waiting for other professionals to become involved, nursery staff suggested to her parents that home and school should introduce Muneeza to some basic Makaton vocabulary and signing skills. Her older brother had attended nursery in the previous academic year and had learnt the rudiments of Makaton signing alongside a little boy with Down syndrome. Amidst the confusion of all the new information concerning their daughter's disability, here was a small element which felt familiar.

At the heart of all curriculum development in the early years is the notion of learning through play (Moyles 1994, David 1996), yet play needs to be tempered by an understanding of the social dimensions of interdependent living and learning (Boyd 1989). Such opportunities must be offered to our 'special' children and their families. There is a tendency to assume that individual input is somehow more appropriate for children with an SEN. However, this can lead to an over-emphasis on one-to-one, adult-to-child curriculum delivery. While this may support skills-based learning, it denies children the opportunity to develop their social and independence skills in an appropriate, interactive, interdependent setting.

It is difficult to imagine what this 'ordinary' nursery year must mean to a family who have spent their child's infancy working alongside paediatricians, health visitors, speech therapists, physiotherapists and pre-school teachers. The accepted norms of parenthood and family life have been changed, challenged and confused by the need to care for their disabled child. At nursery, they can briefly become an 'ordinary' family, attending their local school, following the familiar pattern established by the traditions of their neighbourhood.

Early years practitioners need to be confident about their ability to offer a quality play environment to *all* children (DES 1990), and to be assertive in articulating this curriculum, so that all families find their own place within the nursery and can in turn feel empowered to articulate their needs.

Home: the context for learning

The teacher who works alongside families who have a child with a significant developmental delay needs to acknowledge that parents are in the process of adapting their understanding of the world they and their child are sharing. The parents' initial response to the disclosure of diagnosis can often disrupt their ability to interact in an intuitive and instinctive way with their child, and the normal parent–child relationship is disrupted.

While it is important to recognise that individual responses will be different, parents may feel that the child needs a special approach and that they do not have the appropriate skills to help their child. They may find it difficult to make sense of their child's world and feel they have no model on which to build. They can be apprehensive that they will need different and special skills and that the activities they would normally engage in at home are inappropriate.

Their anxiety is often augmented by parental attempts to initiate play and communication from the earliest weeks of their child's life. All parents wait for their child's first smile, which reinforces the bonding process (Trevarthen 1992). If this response is delayed, the parents may give up their attempts at eliciting responses and stop communicating with the baby. When this natural process is disrupted, it reinforces their feeling that the relationship with the child will be different. It is often at this time that the observations of a health visitor or home teacher with a depth of knowledge about early childhood development is of the greatest value: someone who can say, 'Look, he's not smiling now, but he will. Keep going.'

Jane was happy and excited about the imminent birth of her second child. She had enjoyed all the early stages with her first daughter and felt she was an 'experienced mother'. The second baby, Ann, was born with a disability diagnosed within the first two weeks after birth. The baby slept for most of the day, was difficult to feed and was unresponsive to her attempts to make eye contact and to initiate play. She decided that her best course was to allow Ann to sleep and to concentrate her efforts on Ann's physical needs, in particular her feeding. With the help of a home visitor, Jane and the family were encouraged to maintain their efforts to communicate with Ann through talking, touching, singing and all the appropriate stimuli which they had used with their first child. Thus, Jane was given the confidence to persevere with her initial and instinctive approach and to remain positive and understand that her persistence would yield results.

Research has shown that when a family has been given an early diagnosis of disability, this disclosure generally incorporates medical predictions of what the child will do, how s/he will develop or what s/he will become (McKinley 1994). They can be made to feel that all meaningful learning will require access to specialist personnel and equipment, and that their vocabulary is lacking in the new words they hear from professionals and in specialist literature. At this time, it is the best course for anyone working within the family setting to spend time not advising, but listening to learn how the family functions, and evaluating and assessing their needs. It is within a relationship built on mutual trust that the parents and professionals can support each other, for they have different but equivalent expertise. Any intervention must take account of the family dynamics. The views of the family must be respected. Between professional and family, a way must be found which ensures a dialogue is established whereby learning programmes are developed for the needs of the child and are adapted to accommodate the unique social and emotional resources of the family.

During the first two-and-a-half years of any child's life, the home setting is the focus for development, and it is within this context that any suggestions must be made. Many parents have been bombarded with literature and over-zealous professionals emphasising the need for constant, structured stimulation and specialist intervention programmes. They can feel that they are not able to give this level of commitment and that these demands are affecting their interactions with other members of the family, whose needs are of equal importance. Such demands from professional support workers can be regarded as unrealistic, for 'the baby has come to live with you, not you with the baby' (health visitor).

While the additional professional input is welcome, it tends to set the family apart. In order to counteract this sense of separation, the curriculum must be adapted to the family and not vice versa. Unless care is given to ensure an holistic view of the child's development, feelings of guilt can emerge when the family feels it is unable to achieve skill-related targets.

During the days immediately following the Warnock Report (DES 1978), there was a perception among early intervention practitioners that if children with disabilities acquired cognitive and independence skills, it would enable them to access the early years curriculum of the mainstream nurseries and playgroups. A behaviourist approach was adopted. Skills were often taught in isolation, with specialist equipment and with the use of errorless teaching techniques and its associated language and methods of recording. This specialist approach ignored the need for play as a natural vehicle of learning for the young child and tended to deskill parents, who believed that their instinctive interactions were of less value.

The over-structuring of play alongside the perceived need for the child to extend their skills became an overriding aim within the home setting. Consequently, children entered early years settings able to recognise geometric shape and to match and sort formally, but at a loss when presented with the development of early representational play. Thus, the process of sorting cars by colour or size became more important than watching them shoot down a slope or along a track. Sadly, one teacher from an early intervention team was reported as deciding not to use cars for sorting as 'they distract children from the task; they only want to play'.

In many programmes, the learning outcomes were well-defined and each skill was broken down into its component parts; the only outcomes considered to be of value were those which were measurable. Programmes were drawn up to teach children to match red spoons to red cups, and this became the carefully measured and recorded outcome, rather than an outcome which occurred naturally through involvement in imaginative role play. It was felt that children could not learn these skills incidentally, but that every skill they acquired needed careful preparation and teaching. Such an approach resulted in children becoming dependent on individual adult support; they became unable to complete any given task without the supportive encouraging presence of an adult.

> John's mother was very anxious that his skills should develop, and favoured formal activities. John liked to help his mother with the shopping. He knew where she put the tins – in the cupboard – and where she put the vegetables – under the sink. Through discussion with his home teacher, she allowed time for John to help with the putting away, having been reassured that he was 'matching and sorting'. She recognised the quality of interaction which occurred between them when they talked about the contents, the different sizes of boxes and tins, the weights, the positioning and the sorting opportunities which could not be achieved in the formal presentation of 'big bricks' and 'little bricks'.

Parents are often unaware of their own abilities and the curriculum they offer in their homes. The everyday household activities of dusting and hoovering, of standing at the sink washing up, sorting out the washing or putting the potatoes into the pan can be overlooked in the search for specialist activities. It is the role of the supporting professional to act as an outside observer, identifying learning opportunities and promoting confidence.

> Coralin lived with her mother in her grandparents' home. One day, when the home teacher arrived, she was greeted by a very dirty, muddy child. The grandparents were the carers for the day and were very apologetic about Coralin's appearance. They explained she had been having a wonderful time helping her grandfather in the garden and had not wanted to come indoors, but as the teaching session was 'so important' they would make her. The home visitor decided the best thing to do was to join the gardening group. She participated in the activity and observed the interaction between Coralin and her grandfather: 'You put the apples in this box. I'll put the leaves in my wheelbarrow.... No, not in the wheelbarrow – apples in the box... That is a big apple. Put it in the box....' The direction, interaction and activity lasted for some time longer. Despite Coralin's grandparents' protestations about a waste of a visit, the home visitor was able to share her enthusiasm for what she had seen.

No formal situation, however well-designed, could have encouraged the child's motivation to sort so effectively with such sustained concentration. This was active learning at its most ecologically appropriate.

Parents often need help to recognise the significant role they play as educators within the home. They feel they are 'only playing' with their children. They may need a knowledgeable practitioner to articulate the developmental stages the child is moving through and to demystify the process of learning. The partnership should enable the curriculum which is available in the home throughout each day to merge with the formal needs of child development and to reinforce the natural instinctive relationship between children and their families.

Conclusion

Every family thinks their children special. Every family develops its own culture and shared meanings which its members construct together, whether that involves pet names, 'rituals' ('We always have to go to say goodnight to the cat before going up to bed'), 'bugging and nudging' ('Go on, sing that nursery rhyme for Grandma'), favourite people, television programmes, music, foods, places, outings and so on. Parents and carers know the children more intimately than a teacher can but teachers bring to the partnership expertise developed through their initial and continuous professional education and training, as well as through their experience with a wide range of children and families. They have the knowledge to recognise the patterns (the similarities) in children's development and learning and the surprises (the differences). Both parents/carers and educators, like the children who bring them together, have a need for respect from each other and from society. Every child, every parent or carer, and every teacher needs to feel that what they contribute to the collective learning endeavour is meaningful and valued.

Note

1. Education is here defined as 'appropriate opportunities addressing individual children's developmental and learning needs'.

Chapter 12

Transdisciplinary approaches to working with families

Barbara Doyle

Introduction

In recent years practitioners in early intervention have been challenged with enormous changes in the theoretical and practical, legislative and societal demands placed upon them which provide the framework for their practice. It is a testimony to the commitment of the professionals choosing to work in this field that we have come so far in our efforts to provide comprehensive, caring and respectful support for the families with a child who has special needs. However, as suggested by Shonkoff and Meisels (1990), although the field is a model of remarkable accomplishment, it is also one of unfulfilled opportunity. Much remains to be done and the professionals are faced with many challenges.

Most prominent of the changes we are trying to come to terms with has been the shift in fundamental assumptions about the purpose of early intervention. Traditionally practitioners focused on individual intervention by professionals from different disciplines, and parental involvement was minimal. However, over the last decade, we have seen a major shift in purpose to the support of the whole family.

This reconceptualisation of early intervention has been widely described in the USA by leaders in the field who have developed concepts of parent empowerment and enablement (Dunst 1985, Dunst *et al.* 1988) and family-focused intervention (Bailey *et al.* 1986). Two major tenets have emerged:

- the child can be fully understood only within the context of the family;
- no one agency can meet the diverse and complex needs of the children with special needs and their families, therefore a team approach is necessary.

This reconceptualization was seen to require considerable changes to service delivery (Able-Boone *et al.* 1992, Bailey *et al.* 1992a, Beckman *et al.* 1995, McBride *et al.* 1993, McGonigel *et al.* 1991): 'An enabling approach to working with families requires that professionals re-examine traditional roles and practices and develop new ones which promote mutual respect and partnership' (McGonigel 1991, p. 49).

The focus of change was on parent–professional partnership, and a number of models emerged to provide a framework for understanding and improving practice: the consumer model (Cunningham and Davis 1985), the empowerment model (Appleton and Minchom 1991) and the negotiating model (Dale 1996). I would suggest that in seeking to provide cohesive services to families, we need to address not only true partnership with parents but also true partnership between professionals. This view is shared by Cunningham and Davis (1985) who suggest that in principle such partnerships should be the same as with parents. Each member of the team brings his/her own expertise and complementary skills and has equal status.

In the USA the change to a family-centred approach was embodied in legislation – Public Law 99–457. Central to this is the IFSP. Among the key principles underlying the IFSP process is that family and professional collaboration are the keys to successful intervention. In the USA, an IFSP Expert Team and Task Force were convened to provide guidelines for best practice. They advised that: 'The same paradigm that underlies the family centred IFSP philosophy – that of empowerment and partnership – should direct the construction of a comprehensive, interagency, interdisciplinary early intervention system' (McGonigel *et al.* 1991, p. 53). There are enormous difficulties in implementing this, not least of which is the question of how agencies can coordinate services based on shared philosophies, and how families should be involved in every aspect of service delivery, be it assessment, therapeutic or educational programmes, child-care, family support or team meetings (Bailey *et al.* 1992a).

It may be argued that we already have inter-agency cooperation but it is also fair to say that this is operationalised to varying degrees, with some teams paying lip service to placing family needs first. Professional partnership is expressed through 'team approaches' and, as with parent–professional partnership, there are several models to inform practice. If we desire to be truly family-centred we should aspire to the transdisciplinary approach. The purpose of this chapter is to examine this approach, to understand its development in theory and its application in practice both in UK and further afield and to explore both its potential and difficulties in providing a framework for improvement in service delivery.

Team approaches

As previously stated there are various models of team organisation, and the terms 'multidisciplinary', 'interdisciplinary' and 'transdisciplinary' are familiar and frequently used, often interchangeably. However, we must be mindful that these terms actually represent different ways of thinking and behaving (Foley 1990). It is worth exploring the differences in order to elucidate the rationale for adopting the transdisciplinary approach in true family-centred intervention. Models of teamwork have been described by many authors but I have drawn principally on the writing of Bergen (1994), Cotton (1984), Dale (1996) and Foley (1990).

Multidisciplinary team (MDT)

This approach was developed earlier in this century as medical practice became more specialised and new disciplines emerged. Professionals work in parallel but with little interaction or exchange of information. Assessment by such a team is discipline-specific, each professional assessing on separate occasions. Separate reports are produced and submitted to the team head who synthesises a prescription of recommendations which may or may not reflect the group consensus. The family plays no significant role except to answer questions directed by the professionals who set the agenda. Foley (1990) reminds us that this approach was developed for adults and not for addressing the complex developmental stage of the infant or young child. Ester Cotton (1984) maintains that: 'The MDT does not recognize in practice the global development of the child and perpetuates a linear fragmented approach to treatment and learning, and the division among therapists' (p. 250). This division can result in confusion and insecurity for parents if they are presented with conflicting priorities. Multiple professional visitors or appointments can prove exhausting, invasive and stressful (Beckman *et al.* 1996). If we accept the notion of respectful and caring partnership as a prerequisite to successful intervention, the MDT approach presents considerable barriers.

Interdisciplinary team (IDT)

This approach extends beyond the working in parallel which characterises the MDT towards a more cooperative effort between disciplines and recognises that no single discipline can provide all the answers. However, practitioners still assess individually and consider how the child might benefit from discipline-specific intervention. The team come together to present their individual findings and do attempt to reach some sort of consensus about intervention goals. Each specialist communicates with other members of the team sharing information across the disciplines. However, the implementation of the goals set is still undertaken by individual disciplines. Unlike the MDT, the IDT approach places some emphasis on partnership with parents, and allows and invites involvement.

The IDT approach has considerably more to offer than the MDT and is probably the model which will be most familiar to practitioners in the UK, where variations of it are applied in Child Development or Family Centres and by 'home visiting' services where a variety of professionals from different services try to coordinate a team approach through inter-agency communications and joint case management meetings. A notable example of the interdisciplinary team approach is the Honeylands Family Support Unit serving the Exeter area. This team, developed within a district general hospital paediatric service, has been functioning for many years and exemplifies a 'district handicap team', recommended as a service delivery approach in *Fit for the Future* (Department of Health and Social Security (DHSS) 1976). This report recommended 'a co-ordinated service of care, therapy and education' and the provision of a 'single identifiable source of skilled advice'. The Honeylands Team approach is described fully by Brindlecombe and Russell (1988). The team plans and reviews its programmes together with parents, and a 'named person' or 'key worker' is nominated to be the main link with the family and to provide continuity and cohesion of the programme provided by various members of the team.

A similar interdisciplinary team approach is applied at the KIDS Family Centres, the first of which was set up in London in 1979. The Centres, although all operating flexibly to meet their local community needs, share basic features. These are: the use of a 'named person'; shared control and information; and diversity of parental participation (Dale 1996). In this highly developed model of the IDT, it is an accepted premise that parents and professionals will negotiate participation and roles, and allowance is made for the resolution of conflict. Negotiation is the main decision-making process between team members and between parents and professionals.

Transdisciplinary team (TDT)

The TDT approach developed in response to the changes previously described in early intervention principles and ideas on best practice. A new approach was required to accommodate the belief that the child could not be viewed in isolation from his/her developmental context – the family – and that his/her development in the physical, cognitive and social domains were interdependent and complex. Unlike the previous models the TDT model of team organisation was specifically developed to meet the principles of family-centred early intervention. Bergen (1994) drawing on the work of Foley (1990) summarises the theoretical rationale behind the TDT approach:
- multiple factors converge to produce a given symptom complex;
- the child can be understood only within the context of his social and familial environment;
- all domains are affected because of the global nature of development (i.e. there are domino or cross-over effects);
- there are cumulative adversity effects.

A rationale for the practice of the TDT approach may be summarised as follows:
- different disciplinary perspectives are embedded in an ecological perspective on the child within his/her family to produce a complex but relevant development picture;
- such an integrated approach should be free of professional contradictions and, therefore, of confusion;
- the emphasis on the child within the family context is more meaningful to parents and is potentially more empowering;
- the process allows for significant professional development (explaining your own perspective deepens knowledge and understanding, as does understanding another perspective, and increases the potential for effectiveness).

These principles of theory and practice complement the principles of family-centred intervention. But what are the critical operational features of this approach which define it as being most congruent with 'best practice'? In 1976 the United Cerebral Palsy Association in the USA (cited in Foley 1990) described the transdisciplinary approach as:

'a deliberate pooling and exchange of information, knowledge and skills, and the crossing and recrossing of traditional disciplinary boundaries by various team members' (Foley 1990, p. 274). The critical word here is 'deliberate'. In the TDT approach the pooling and exchange is operationalised and not left to chance.

Critical features of the transdisciplinary approach

The critical features are *role release, role expansion, arena evaluation* and *selection of a primary provider*. These features identify a transdisciplinary team in its truest sense. However, some of these features are recognisable in teams which do not identify themselves as fully transdisciplinary and reference will be made to them as illustrations of transdisciplinary team features operating in the real world.

Role release

This is the process by which team members transfer specific skills and techniques to other team members to provide integrated intervention through one primary worker. It goes beyond the sharing of information because, as Ester Cotton (1984) describes, the TDT aims at integration where a team member will take on aspects of another member's job so that one suitable worker can be chosen to work to all goals. It requires the renunciation of all professional jealousies and regular training over time. Role release may appear to be threatening to many practitioners, but it was never the intention of the model that some children would not require individual therapy at certain times and the model is based on mutual respect for disciplinary-specific skills.

Role expansion

In role expansion team members 'elaborate' their specific knowledge across disciplines. It occurs in the TDT approach when team members train each other in the concepts of their own disciplines. The aim is not for everyone to be the same but to retain individuality within a meshing of knowledge in order to provide the family with a unity in intervention. Role expansion requires the development of common understanding and language use which are seen as strengthening the ability of the team to provide cohesion and reduce confusion. According to Bergen (1994, p. 245), 'This exchange of roles is the process that separates transdisciplinary teams from other models.'

It is obvious that role release and expansion are not easy to achieve. They will require changes both in the way people operate at a personal level and also in the management structures which are most typically hierarchical in nature. In the TDT, management needs to be circular or collegiate in style.

Arena evaluation

This feature defines the assessment mode of the transdisciplinary model. Assessment is a key feature of any intervention programme and is the area where, certainly in the UK, much designated teamwork is focused. Arena evaluation means that professionals in the team *simultaneously* assess the child. In most scenarios, team members individually assess the child and then try to bring their assessments together. In the TDT, the team design one assessment 'window', a common sample of behaviour that the team can use to observe and collect the information they need to plan integrated goals for intervention. This reflects the holistic view of overlapping development and symptom complexes in the child. In practice, once the scenario for assessment is decided (e.g. a play situation where several activities will demonstrate chosen functions), one professional will do the assessment with others assisting or observing the areas their discipline focuses upon. Most assessment still relies heavily on discipline-specific instruments, so considerable effort is required to design and operationalise the assessment.

Foley (1990) offers us a possible framework. He suggests that each practitioner identifies the essential information s/he requires and outlines the sample of behaviour which might be used. The team together construct an outline of categories and review a sample of instruments to find one which 'contains the broadest outline pool'. Many assessment schedules duplicate items, e.g. handling blocks. This would become the core assessment instrument, and the team would elaborate this by selecting sections from other instruments. Attention is paid to making the environment secure, warm and naturalistic. In this environment, the team may choose to observe feeding, changing, play, language, social interaction, separation or formal tasks.

The role of parents

In the ideal model the parents are seen as equal status partners, holding the key to successful intervention. Parents are provided with full information on team members and their backgrounds. Ideally they are involved in identifying assessment needs and in the assessment and development of the outcome plans. Their knowledge of the child and his/her needs within the context of their family are given equal weight. They are involved at their chosen level in assessment rather than being recipients of its outcome. They have the opportunity to view the same sample of behaviour and be involved in its selection, to act as comforters for their child, and have an opportunity to optimise their performance. As Foley (1990, p. 279) puts it: 'Parents add enormously to the reliability and validity of the evaluation, for ultimately they know their child best.' Fuller descriptions of the model may be found in Foley (1990) and Bergen (1994).

An excellent example of this type of arena evaluation operating in the UK is the pre-school assessment model (PRESAM) developed by members of the Brent Educational Psychology Service (Smith *et al.* 1996). Although described as a multidisciplinary model, operationally it mirrors the simultaneous assessment of arena evaluation. Parents are centrally involved throughout this process and the authors report that PRESAM 'reflected a response to parental frustration at being passed on from one professional to another and being "told nothing" or worse still being told many different things' (Smith *et al.* 1996, p. 3). Apart from enabling better partnership with parents, the authors report a 'feel good' factor among professionals involved, as they found collaborating in family support reduced family anxiety. They add that during the sessions, professionals were rarely seen to disagree, and this was also leading to further cooperation in areas other than assessment.

Selection of a primary provider

The primary provider is at the crux of service delivery in the TDT approach. They are selected by the team, including the parents, as the most appropriate person to work with a particular family. Like a key worker or named person, they act as the coordinator and link person between the family and the team, but they take this role a step further. The primary provider delivers with the parents a unified programme addressing the physical, cognitive and social development of the child and the needs of the family. They need to be trained in those aspects which are outside their disciplinary domain. They are the receivers of role release and need to acknowledge when to draw on discipline specific knowledge. The members who release their roles do retain responsibility for those aspects through the overall responsibility of the whole team for the programme. This immediately draws attention to the level of trust which is required of transdisciplinary team members.

Clearly the demands of this approach are great, and achieving the trust, understanding and high levels of communication and negotiation required is a long and difficult process. From examples of attempts by teams to adopt this approach, we can identify a number of critical issues for success.

Critical issues for success

Adopting a transdisciplinary approach requires changes at system support, team and individual member levels. Change in practice is notoriously difficult to achieve, and the greater the magnitude of change, the more difficult it is.

Support for change

It has already been mentioned that teamwork was supported in the USA: through legislation and guidance from the IFSP Expert Team and Task Force (offering strategies for ensuring inter-agency practice at a local level and recognising the importance of the training of personnel for partnership both with parents and each other); through a limited amount of efficacy research dictating best practice (Bailey *et al.* 1992b); and through current beliefs and values regarding approaches (McBride *et al.* 1993).

In the USA then, we see there is specific legislation in support of family-centred and collaborative teamwork aspiring to at least most aspects of the transdisciplinary approach. In New Zealand, there have also been significant attempts to support family-centred practice through legislation for special education. Twiss *et al.* (this volume), describing the current provision for early intervention services, indicates how recent legislation in New Zealand places an emphasis on the 'availability of specialist staff working collaboratively across disciplines and agencies to provide a range of service provision including transdisciplinary teams' and that increased funding in the last few years has been made available to achieve this.

In the UK, legislation and government directives associated with the major service providers have long supported the concept of teamwork (DoH 1991, DES 1978, DfE 1994, DHSS 1976, Education Act 1981, Younghusband *et al.* 1970). Despite this rhetorical support, teamwork has not developed to the same degree in the UK, and the term 'trans-disciplinary' seems to arouse a degree of negativity and suspicion among some practitioners. The Court Report (DHSS 1976) found that practitioners were not well-disposed to cooperate and collaborate, nor was the framework for its facilitation available in most areas. Some 20 years on these issues seem to remain. Even where there is the will and commitment to work with other disciplines the framework for its facilitation has not been addressed. Rhetoric has not been supported by appropriate resources for practice, research or the training needs implicated.

Commitment to a principle

Legislation alone can never produce true change without the will and commitment of the practitioners. In my own case, commitment to the approach has grown entirely from direct experience. As a young teacher in a residential special school, I was fortunate to experience the benefits of working collaboratively, initiated quite by chance when one morning the speech therapist was unable to work in her own room and asked to work in mine. The experience for us was so positive that we set about a complete reorganisation of our work to accommodate our new approach, supported by a flexible and insightful headteacher who was prepared to facilitate us. The success of our intervention with our young children drew the interest of other therapies into collaboration, and I began to join them on their home visits in the holidays. With will and commitment, a close relative of the transdisciplinary approach operated for the youngest children in the school, and my commitment to full collaboration was secured.

In researching this chapter I discussed the approach with the directors of two very different centres in the UK where I believed I had recognised teamwork equating with, or exhibiting aspects of, the transdisciplinary approach: the Hornsey Centre for children with cerebral palsy in London and one of the KIDS Family Centres in Birmingham. Both directors expressed similar experiences to mine and supported the notion that commitment and positive attitude were crucial to effective teamwork. Just bringing people together and designating them as a team will not ensure collaboration. Commitment to a shared set of principles is necessary. Perhaps it is important to note that both centres are based on strongly held beliefs which staff must share.

The Hornsey Centre is a centre for conductive education. (It is not the concern of this chapter to debate this as an intervention, but to explore aspects of transdisciplinary teamwork which can be illustrated by the work of the Hornsey team.) The programme sees itself as holistic and naturalistic as normal daily activities are used to plan the learning programme and the parents must be fully involved in helping the child to practise and learn in different activities. Staff applying to work there come from a variety of different educational and therapeutic backgrounds but must commit themselves to training as a conductor. In doing so, they clearly experience role release and expansion to become what is, in essence, a primary provider, albeit of a specific type of intervention. The conductor teaches the child all skills and replaces the many professional people usually involved and is hence closely akin to the 'primary provider'.

Role release and expansion are probably the most difficult issues to address in developing a transdisciplinary team. Teams such as the one at Hornsey are advantaged in achieving this by selecting staff clearly committed to the approach and its role requirements. Similarly Dale (1996) describes how staff choosing to work at KIDS must commit to training in additional skills, Portage Home Teaching, counselling, communication and negotiation. There are other difficulties associated with team delivery which are associated with bringing different disciplines together. Professional jealousies, different conditions of service, differentials in pay, working hours and holidays can be detrimental to team harmony. In times of economic constraint, some professionals may well fear that in releasing some aspect of your role to another there is a danger of 'doing oneself out of a job'. Although many see the prospect as an exciting learning opportunity, others see it as a dangerous dilution of hard-earned expertise.

The context

Perhaps it is an important distinction that both the Hornsey Centre and KIDS Family Centres operate in cooperation with, but are outside, the statutory education, health and social services. This enables them to achieve a consensus in philosophy through selection and training. Dale (1996), in describing the team at the KIDS Centre, London, also upholds this 'consensus in philosophy and approach permitting a consistency in practice in working with parents and families' (p. 287).

In those teams made up of individuals assigned from community services, professionals have the difficulty of divided loyalties. They may wish to operate in a particular way within the team but must also pay attention to the demands of their line managers in the discipline-based services. Resource and responsibility interests may compete and work against the cohesion of the team. At the KIDS Family Centre and the Hornsey Centre, they have management structures designed to facilitate and promote teamwork through underpinning principles to respect and learn from the exchange of knowledge in true collaboration. In many ways a centre-based programme is seen as more appropriate and unfragmented (Dale 1996). Ayshe Talay-Ongan (1991) describes the operation of a centre-based transdisciplinary team at the Centre for the Competent Child in California. It facilitates the transdisciplinary approach by creating structures and opportunities for professionals to work together and learn from each other, and by facilitating meeting for joint planning and coordination. It is much more difficult to achieve when professionals are visiting homes separately and reporting only to each other. However, in the USA it was seen as one of the positive outcomes of the approach that in rural areas, for example, where parents were unable to attend a centre, the use of a transdisciplinary team primary provider would be both beneficial to the family and a more cost-effective service, while reducing the intrusion on the family.

Operational frameworks

It has already been suggested that commitment to shared principles and strategies are crucial to transdisciplinary teamwork. An operational framework which fosters these is equally important. Bergen (1994) emphasises that the operational framework needs to facilitate communication, team building activities, professional preparation and conflict resolution. In building a successful TDT, these issues cannot be assumed to evolve on their own, they must be systematically planned and provided for. This is one of the difficulties faced by many professionals trying to function in teams. Addressing team issues is never a priority for resources, in terms of time allowed to meet, discuss and train together. The critical importance of staff preparation and in-service training is identified by several authors (Bailey *et al.* 1992a,

Beckman 1996, Cotton 1984, McGonigel *et al.* 1991, Smith 1995). In her discussion on preparing early intervention professionals, Beckman refers to the need to understand the role and contribution of other team members; to have the ability to negotiate and define roles for all members; to understand team dynamics and how 'turf' issues or interpersonal issues influence the functioning of the team and of the effects of these on families. For the TDT at the Centre for the Competent Child, communication, sharing and in-service training were made a priority in the administration of services (Talay-Ongan 1991). Every fourth week, one of the weekly clinical meetings was scheduled for staff development led by a team member.

Collaboration with other disciplines to some degree is now a part of almost every practitioner's role, yet little attention is given to this in either initial or in-service training. Professionals are not well prepared for this important aspect of their work. Time must be allowed for teams of professionals to address team dynamics and the question of how they can come to treat parents as full partners. McGonigel *et al.* (1991) point out the merits of including parents in training programmes and of providing joint training opportunities. Many service professionals who believe they are engaged in partnership with parents fail to address this issue. We must recognise the need to learn from and with our parent partners.

Equality for parents in the decision-making process is central to the transdisciplinary approach. Equality here should be synonymous with opportunity to decide. Parents will wish to take an active part in decision-making to varying degrees and at different times in the life cycle of intervention. They must be allowed to choose this level for themselves (Able-Boone *et al.* 1992) in a true partnership.

Conclusion

Working in a transdisciplinary team way is a great challenge to all of us who wish to continue the improvement of service provision through professional collaboration. It raises questions about service delivery and the need for flexibility with respect for the needs and constraints on all those involved.

Transdisciplinary team working is not only about procedures for service delivery, it is about values and attitudes of respect for different perspectives and a willingness or even desire to share knowledge to improve our practice for the good of those we seek to help. It is about the development of practitioners who adopt family-centred rather than service-centred approaches.

We need to be able to learn from situations at home and abroad and to see what we can absorb and adapt into our own systems, protocols and cultural framework. This would be best done for practitioners by practitioners and in a transdisciplinary way. A tall order! Yes, but the positive changes that have occurred in the provision for children with disabilities and their families have happened because of the commitment of reflective practitioners with vision who strove to work for improvement when they recognised the need.

Transdisciplinary intervention will not provide solutions to all of the service difficulties faced by professionals and parents, but it 'may serve to improve assessment methods, to demonstrate the truth of the Gestalt principle that the "whole is greater than the sum of its parts", and to give young children their best chance of getting the range of prevention and intervention services' (Bergen 1994, p. 9).

I believe that the parents of the children we work with have taught us a great deal about effort and commitment. We have expected much of them, and I suggest we need to keep listening to what they have to say about how we work with them. In the words of a parent, 'we need to reduce the stakes and be able to work together in a spirit of real partnership without allowing issues of power, control and privilege to interfere with what we have come to do' (Manuel 1996, p. 3).

Chapter 13

Moving forward together: collaborative research with families

Barry Carpenter

Introduction

The message of this chapter is simple: if we are truly to empower parents then we, as professionals representing a variety of disciplines, must be prepared to 'let go'. The multiplicity of strategies proposed by professionals during the 'parenting years' necessitates constant decision-making and conflict resolution on the part of the parents. An over-reliance on professional input can disempower parents, cause feelings of inadequacy, and encourage the tendency to problem-solve only when supported by professionals.

These are undesirable traits if families are to lead full and meaningful lives. We often talk of 'partnership with parents' from the professional perspective, but however 'consumerist' or interactive our patterns of partnership may be, they always carry our professional bias. If we are truthful, where does the balance of 'power' lie?

Through three pieces of recent research, not all of which were directly related to this theme, I began to realise that many parents, for a variety of positive and negative reasons, were beginning to take control: they were identifying needs within their family, planning their intervention strategy, putting this into action, and then reflecting upon the outcomes before making further modifications of the original plan. I will return to this cycle later in the chapter after considering the research history which has led to the development of the 'parent as researcher' paradigm.

Firstly, recent research with fathers of children with disabilities (Carpenter and Herbert 1995b, Herbert and Carpenter 1994) revealed that families had evolved their own networking structures. These provided sources of information and support which either compensated for knowledge parents had not gained from professionals or enabled parents to make sense of information they had been given.

Secondly, a comparative study of three early intervention programmes in New Zealand, Australia and the UK (Carpenter this volume), which identified indicators of good practice, showed that, in effective practice models, parents were not only integral to the whole operation of family-focused service delivery, but were also seen as service deliverers themselves. There was a recognition of their unique and invaluable contribution and their capacity to manage difficult situations, often using only the resources (physical, human and material) available within their own family.

A third piece of research focused on the attitudes of mainstream 7–8-year-olds to a peer with Down syndrome (Carpenter 1995d). Unlike earlier research on this theme (Lewis 1995), the outcomes of this research were interpreted in terms of family empowerment within a community, following a positive period of interaction for the child with Down syndrome in a neighbourhood school setting. This case study demonstrated how proactive the parents had been in securing, supporting and sustaining the placement in a neighbourhood school for their child, and that they had been both instigator and catalyst for this initiative, coordinating professional inputs as needed to achieve their family goals.

In each of these three research studies, there was evidence of parents investigating, enquiring, discovering information, planning, delivering services, monitoring and evaluating. Quality in parental involvement remains a vexed issue, and several researchers are seeking to evolve effective models (Dale 1996, Hornby 1989). Some are articulating the case for parental empowerment (Dempsey 1993). All share the goal of improving the quality of parents' (and families') interactions with a variety of personnel linked to a child with a disability. All suggest that a diverse repertoire of involvement strategies will be needed to accommodate the obvious differences that exist between all families (Hornby 1995). However, none has suggested that some parents may wish to act as the researcher, to gain their own insights into their child and family needs through investigation and enquiry which will illuminate the patterns of interaction. For some parents, this may generate some insight for answers to the deep and vexing questions they often have and which some professionals find perplexing and are unable to resolve. Thus, I decided to explore further the 'parent as researcher' paradigm.

Family involvement

Blackstone and Williams (1994) illustrate how professionals often blame the family for the failures of their educational, health and welfare systems. Apportionment of blame is often mutual: it inevitably occurs where, maybe due to lack of resources, professionals feel that they have not delivered an adequate service to a family; or, conversely, where parents feel that their agenda has not been addressed by the professionals.

Shotter (1993) states:

> No matter how benevolent we may be towards those we study – no matter how concerned we are with 'their' liberation, with 'their' betterment, the fact is that we do not make sense of 'their' lives in 'their' terms.

> (p. 48)

So how do we make better sense for families of their lives? Surely to achieve this professionals must relinquish some of their domination of early intervention programmes (Basil 1994b) and invest the power in the parents who can then control their own situation, their own lives and the lives of their children by accessing professional resources at times when they feel it to be valuable. This approach would give both advocacy and empowerment to the parents, and would demand a reconceptualisation of the patterns of working to date. With the ever-shrinking resources available to early intervention, such a model may be the only way forward if we are to continue to give families opportunities, awareness and skills that will benefit their family life.

This particular line of thought would be supported by the empowerment model of working with parents advocated by Appleton and Minchcom (1991). In this approach there is a recognition that a family is a system with its own social network. It echoes the consumer approach (Cunningham and Davis 1985), but clearly states that parents should have a choice of service and of their level of engagement with that service. Recently, this work has been further developed by Dale (1996) through her negotiation model. Her approach, in which the parent was not only seen as an equal, but also as a leader in the parent–professional relationship at certain points, should be fundamental to such working relationships. Dale's model embodies negotiation as a key transaction for partnership which will lead in time to joint decision-making. Through shared perspectives, and the process of mediation, resolution of differences are achieved (or sometimes not!). Perhaps, in the past, our notions of working with parents have been too simplistic. In reality, partnership with parents and families is a multitiered concept.

Lessons from early intervention

For any parent of a child with a disability, the desire to secure a life of dignity for their child is at the heart of their personal motivation for ensuring that their child receives a range of quality services which increase his/her quality of life. But to achieve this, many parents find themselves battling with either service overload or service impoverishment: as service providers, we tend either to give parents too much or too little. In a recent piece of research conducted by an advisory teacher for multisensory impairment, Husbands (1996) writes:

> I was struck by the enormous juggling act that parents are required to perform between appointments, home, work, family life and the needs of other children, as well as the needs of the disabled child. This is a daily reality for many parents; is it any wonder that they feel they are not in control, and as the years pass these feelings may become exacerbated.
>
> (p. 2)

It is valuable to reflect on development in the field of early intervention, and how it has moved to more family-based approaches of service delivery. Such models acknowledge the child's context, for children do not develop separately from this context, but are always in interaction with their environment.

Many researchers and practitioners feel that family-centred models are both more humane and more dignifying to the child and its family. This is not to diminish the qualities that professionals working in the early intervention phase should possess, but to emphasise that the early intervention team should have the family at its centre. As such, this team, even at times of uncertainty and anxiety, should be self-supporting and self-sustaining. Such approaches increase the capacity of families to provide resources to other families to assist in solving problems. Hornby (1989, 1995) has written extensively on parent-to-parent schemes which illustrate this particular approach. Sensitive interaction within the early intervention team will enable a family to change its contribution over a period of time. The dimensions of family involvement may increase or decrease depending on how the family may be feeling at a particular time. As with any child-rearing process, there are problem patches. What we must acknowledge is that families of children with disabilities are first and foremost families, and, while being positive in our focus, there should be space for and acceptance of the full range of emotions experienced by any family.

In Europe, family-centred approaches to early intervention have been the subject of recent research. Peterander (1995) writes that holistic, family-orientated approaches require close collaboration between the range of professionals in the field of pedagogy, psychology, social sciences and medicine. In Finland, Mattus (1994) and Mäki (1994) recommend an ecological approach in which the involvement of the family is pivotal. The purpose of this approach is to gather information about children's real lives: their activities, interactions, experiences and peer contacts in natural environments. The context for early intervention has come under close scrutiny (Pieterse *et al.* 1988). The particular benefit to families of such approaches is that it puts them in a position of control whereby they can access services rather than waiting in a dependent fashion for things to be done to them by various service deliverers. Again, such approaches are not intended to eradicate the contribution of professionals, but rather to define more sharply the role of professionals within the family context, for as Seligman and Darling (1989) state: 'Professionals in families can work to eliminate the physical, cultural and social barriers that prevent families from attaining the best quality of life' (p. 237); 'What is undeniable, is that "parenthood needs support"'(Virpiranta-Sala 1994).

The contribution of research

Much of the research on families with a disabled child has tended to adopt a 'stress and coping' approach. This has been informed by highly developed theoretical models of stress and coping and has been shown to be more predictive of parents'/carers' well-being than the more traditional predictors such as severity of disability and care needs (Quine and Pahl 1991, Sloper *et al.* 1991, Wilton and Renaut 1986). However, skilled researchers in the field of disability and social welfare have begun to realise that such approaches further emphasise the negative aspects of having a disabled member within a family circle. Titterton (1992) has called for 'a new approach which can account for the creative problem-solving of diverse individuals in the face of adversity' (p. 5).

Beresford (1996) has, through her own recent research, developed an approach which, instead of focusing on the negative aspects of caring for a disabled child, has sought to recognise the importance of looking at how parents cope with the difficulties they face. In so doing, she has cast parents in a new role in which they are seen as actively managing this situation. If we do not begin to acknowledge parents in this role, then our understanding of the lives of families caring for a disabled child will remain incomplete.

Links with empowerment

Empowerment is related to an individual's or, in this case, a family's use of their support networks. The process of empowerment is predicated on an ecological understanding of the environment, which includes personal social networks as a key component. Mutual respect between service providers and service receivers is considered critical in the empowering process. This includes an understanding that 'people disadvantaged by the way that society is currently structured, must play a primary role in developing strategies by which they gain increased control over valued resources' (Cochran 1990, p. 54). Dunst *et al.* (1988) provide valuable guidelines associated with enabling and empowering families based on an extensive review of the literature. The constructs they devise could form the basis of valuable research examining the relationship between empowered families, family-focused practices and family self-perceptions of their role. Dempsey (1993) calls for further research to be carried out in this field, particularly using qualitative research techniques. However, his call again falls somewhat short in that it relies upon professionals conducting that research.

It is fascinating to see that people in various parts of the world are beginning to arrive at a similar critical point (Beresford 1996, Dempsey 1993, Nihira *et al.* 1994, Weiser and Gallimore 1994).

Developing a parent-based research role

In advocating new approaches to research which base themselves around family-focused models of service delivery, none of the key researchers and professionals has got quite so far as to suggest that parents themselves should be allowed to take the reins of research. We should of course heed Anderson *et al.*'s warning (1994) that: 'The challenge is to create ways to do research without overwhelming ourselves in the process; to make research an integral part of what we already do, rather than merely an "add on"' (p. 175).

The 'parent as researcher' paradigm is premised on the action research approach. This particular approach is intended to facilitate problem-solving, and has gained particular popularity in research circles in Britain (Robson 1993). Rapoport (1970) stated that: 'action research aims to contribute to the practical concerns of people in an immediate problematic situation' (p. 1). Robson (1993) asserts that improvement and involvement are central to the spiral cycles of action research. This spiral of cycles involves: planning, acting, observing and reflecting. Carr and Kemmis (1986) identify:

> Firstly, the improvement of *practice* of some kind; secondly, the improvement of the *understanding* of practice by its practitioners; and thirdly, the improvement of the *situation* in which the practice takes place. Those involved in the practice being considered are to be involved in the action research process in all its aspects of planning, acting, observing and reflecting.
>
> (p. 165)

How does this apply to families? For them the *practice* is events in the family life cycle and the *practitioners* the family members themselves. The *situation* is the family context: its home – the home being the naturalistic setting advocated by key proponents of family-focused models of service delivery (Noonan and McCormick 1993). The well-documented cycle of planning, acting, observing and reflecting is a process which mirrors the pattern adopted by many families in seeking solutions to family problems or concerns in relation to their child with disability.

The power of the paradigm

The power of this paradigm rests in its ecological validity. The use of natural environments in early intervention has been exalted by researchers and practitioners (Noonan and McCormick 1993), who stress that intervention strategies based on methods used in restrictive clinical settings are neither effective nor practical for children with disabilities and their families. We know that human development and behaviour cannot be understood independently of the social context in which it occurs (Brinker 1992, Hornby 1995). Guralnick (1991) illustrated that the new approaches in early intervention (i.e. those that were family-focused) were firmly grounded in contemporary family systems theory and well-established ecological and developmental models (Bailey and Simeonsson 1984, Bronfenbrenner 1979). However, neither Guralnick nor other proponents of family-focused models of service delivery quite envisaged either that parents themselves might wish to take on the role of researcher or that, at a more fundamental level, professionals should acknowledge the value of parents' direct involvement in the enquiry, exploration and investigation of action research.

The 'parent as researcher' paradigm rests well within the ecocultural model described by Nihira *et al.* (1994). They state:

> The ecocultural model, as applied to families of children with developmental delays, is a comprehensive approach composed of: (a) a context that provides opportunities for and constraints on the families; (b) families' perspectives of their lives and circumstances, including their values and goals; and (c) families' proactive efforts to accommodate the child with developmental delay.
>
> (p. 552)

Taking part (b) of this ecocultural model, instead of the researcher (as an outsider) drawing perspectives from families, the 'parent as researcher' paradigm that I am proposing bestows the role of researcher on the parent; they are the natural enquirer within their family – the seeker of knowledge and information that will illuminate needs within their family and specifically in relation to their child with a disability. If we wish to progress family-focused models of service delivery, then we must evolve parent-inclusive patterns of research. I affirm this not to deny the validity of other types of research, with or about families, or the capacity of this research to extend the body of knowledge; rather, it is to make the statement that if we wish truly to empower parents of children with disabilities, then part of that enabling process must be to offer them, as an option, the role of researcher. We must acknowledge their right to investigate their own family functions; indeed, we must acknowledge that this is already part of the process they engage in as parents. As such, the experiences they accumulate can form a data collection, which they with others may choose to analyse to illuminate the patterns of parenting and family functioning embarked upon when one or more family members have a disability.

From paradigm to practice

The underlying principle of this paradigm is to enable and empower families. This family-focused research dimension mirrors the principles and guidelines for practice offered by authors such as Dunst *et al.* (1988).

Earlier in the chapter, I mentioned that the formation of this paradigm evolved from earlier research experiences. In particular, within the work on fathers (Carpenter and Herbert 1995b, Herbert and Carpenter 1994), the cycle of observation, planning, action and reflection could be found in all of the transcribed data from the interviews with the fathers.

A further ten interviews were constructed with families of children with disabilities who had received early intervention services in the previous two years. Initially, a letter was sent to these families asking if they would be prepared to share one aspect of their life story. When the consent was received from the parents, a further letter was sent prior to a home visit, during which a semi-structured interview was conducted. In the letter prior to the interview, parents were asked to identify an incident within their family, in relation to their child with a disability, where they had, through their observations, made an action plan, implemented that plan and thought about its outcomes. The letter summarised this in a flow diagram (*see* Figure 13.1).

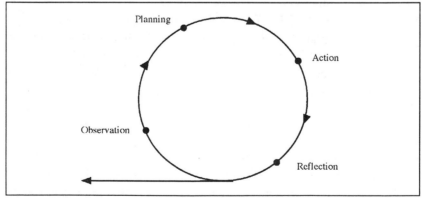

Figure 13.1   Parent enquiry cycle

In all ten cases, parents had said they had experienced that particular cycle and gave ecologically valid reports. Eight parents actually had written evidence of such a process.

A key feature which emerged was that in all ten cases, the action taken by the parents involved their marshalling some professional resource. The basic process seems to have been one of identifying, through observation, a particular need for their child (e.g. speech therapy), then making contact with the relevant professional agency (i.e. what Carpenter (this volume) has termed as 'families pressing the button'). Having made their plan and identified the need then, with the professional concerned, they undertook the necessary action and reflected upon the outcomes of that period of intervention. These examples demonstrate the capacity of many professionals to work effectively alongside parents, and clearly illustrate that we have gone beyond the transplant model of parent–professional relationships that so typified that work in the late 1960s and early 1970s.

Further investigation of the 'parent as researcher' paradigm was made by considering the literature written by parents themselves. There is an incredible wealth of such literature, sadly not always valued by the academic community, which powerfully illustrates, from within the family, the experiences of that family. In the books written by Joan Hebden, Pat Fitton, and Carol Johnson and Julia Crowder, the cycle of observation, planning, action and reflection was again identified, and I would commend these texts to you.

A further literature search looked at the case studies and essays produced either through parent–professional collaboration or initially by parents and then edited by a professional. This gave further insights to the problem-solving and knowledge acquisition processes within families that allow them to meet the needs of their child with a disability. What emerged from this literature search was how this process was also applied to meet the needs of other family members, e.g. siblings, grandparents, etc.

Among the literature sources here were the work of MacWilliam and Bailey (1993), Ballard (1994) and Meyer (1995). Wills (1994) offers, coincidentally, an excellent rationale for the 'parent as researcher' paradigm – 'to see the world that parents experience' (p. 257). He further cites some words of a parent, Lesley Macks, which pinpoint the need to give parents maximum control over their family lives while providing a well-resourced support structure:

> Birth has propelled the whole family into a kind of pinball game, on a course over which you have no control as you fly into contact with this agency or that individual. Sometimes the contact is a profitable one and the lights flash and the score mounts. Sometimes it is counterproductive, causing a noisy clash and flying sparks. And as you hurtle, 'til you come to the roller coaster ride which takes you to the depths, up to hope, even the heights of exaltation, then plunges you down into a black tunnel again before sending you out on to a safe plateau.
>
> (Lesley Macks, cited by Wills 1994, p. 257)

For some parents, the 'parent as researcher' paradigm could offer them an emotional outlet for the pressures of parenting a child with a disability. Nicholas Kappes, describing his experience as a parent in the collection of essays edited by Donald Meyer (1995), writes: 'now, unrelenting stress, constantly sidetracks us, draining our time and energy' (p. 21) and that 'time freezes – then jerks forward' (p. 20). Meyer's series of essays also demonstrates how fathers in particular have engaged in the cycle of observing their children, making plans, taking action and reflecting. At the moment this book would be regarded as a series of essays; is it not equally valid as a source of data?

The 'parent as researcher' paradigm clearly needs to be tested on a wider scale, but there is evidence from existing research, from the literature and from the writings of parents themselves, that we need to take one bold step forward: to acknowledge the direct contribution of parents to the research process, so that they can exercise their choice to become the researcher without fear of recrimination from the research community. This message is a crucial one if we are to advance services in the field of early intervention. In many countries, early intervention resources are under threat as budget cuts bite hard. How do administrators know where to cut? They may turn for advice to researchers – do *we* know? The true and most powerful answer would come from parents themselves: they have 'researched' their own family needs, the needs of their child with a disability. Have we been fair to them? Have we given them a voice in the research: not our voice – their own?

Conclusion

This chapter has sought to expound a new paradigm – that of the 'parent as researcher'. It affirms what many others have stated: that in the field of early intervention, family-focused models are proving to be the most effective. Thus if the research process rests within the family, then the parents must have, if they wish, ownership of that process. This would enrich the field of research in early intervention in that parents would then begin to evolve the research agenda. This would be dynamic and exciting for, as outsiders looking in, we can bring only *our* perceptions and interpretations to the life cycle of the family. From within the family itself, the situation may look very different. Thus the research agenda would comprise issues that were significant and meaningful to the families.

Inevitably, because of their varying backgrounds, many parents choosing to become researchers will need partners in the research process, and this is where professionals still have a very necessary role. In all other forms of partnership with parents, we have been encouraged to adopt a partnership that is equal (Wolfendale 1989). Has this extended to the field of research? However sensitive our practices may have been, have we not, in the past, 'used' parents in our research? They have not been our equal partners, but rather our subjects. Through the collaborative process of sharing and illumination, the quality of life opportunities for families with a disabled family member may be enriched and their needs more effectively met.

References

Able-Boone, H., Sandall, S. R., Gordon, N. and Martin, D. G. (1992) 'Consumer based early intervention services', *Journal of Early Intervention,* **16** (3), 201–209.

Amin, K. and Oppenheim, C. (1992) *Poverty in Black and White.* London: The Runnymede Trust.

Anderson, G., Herr, K. and Nihlen, A. (1994) *Studying your own School: An Educator's Guide to Qualitative Practitioner Research,* London: Sage.

Appleton, P. L. and Minchom, P. E. (1991) 'Models of parent partnership and child development centres', *Child: Care, Health and Development,* **17**, 27–38.

Ardito, M., Damiani, M. and Freeman, S. (1994) 'Demographics of users of case management and their perception of natural support', paper presented to American Association of Mental Retardation 118th Annual Meeting, Boston, USA.

Atkins, S. (1994) 'Empowering parents to act as partners in planning for their differently able children', paper presented to the international seminar on 'Partnership between Parents and Professionals in the Care of Children and Young People with Learning Disabilities', UMIST, Manchester, UK.

Atkinson, N. and Crawforth, M. (1995) *All in the Family: Siblings and Disability.* London: NHC Action for Children.

Audit Commission (1994) *Seen but not Heard: Co-ordinating Child Health and Social Services for Children in Need.* London: HMSO.

Bailey, D. B. and Simeonsson, R. J. (1984) 'Critical issues underlying research and intervention with families of young handicapped children', *Journal of the Division for Early Childhood,* **9**, 38–48.

Bailey, D. B. and Simeonsson, R. J. (1988) 'Assessing needs of families with handicapped infants', *Journal of Special Education,* **22**, 117–27.

Bailey, D. B., Buysse, V., Edmondson, R. and Smith, T. M. (1992a) 'Creating family-centred services in Early Intervention: perceptions of professionals in four states', *Exceptional Children,* **58** (4), 298–309.

Bailey, D. B., McWilliam, P. J. and Winton, P. J. (1992b) 'Building family-centred practices in Early Intervention: a team-based model for change', *Infants and Young Children,* **5** (1), 73–82.

Bailey, D. B., Palsha, S. A. and Huntington, G. S. (1990) 'Preservice preparation of special educators to work with infants with handicaps and their families: current status and training needs', *Journal of Early Intervention,* **14** (1), 43–54.

Bailey, D. B. *et al.* (1986) 'Family-focused intervention: a functional model for planning, implementing, and evaluating individualised family services in Early Intervention', *Journal of the Division for Early Childhood,* **10**, 156–71.

Ball, I. (1996) 'Drugs fear for unborn babies', *Sunday Times,* (20 October).

Ballard, K. (ed.) (1994) *Disability, Family, Whānau and Society.* Palmerston North, NZ: Dunmore Press.

Bank, S. P. and Kahn, M. D. (1982) *The Sibling Bond.* New York: Basic Books.

Barnett, W. S. and Boyce, G. C. (1995) 'Effects of children with Down syndrome on parents' activities', *American Journal on Mental Retardation,* **100** (2), 115–27.

Basil, C. (1994a) 'Family involvement in the intervention process', in Broding, J. and Bjorck-Akesson, E. (eds) *Methodological Issues in Research in Augmentative and Alternative*

Communication. Jonkoping: Jonkoping University Press.

Basil, C. (1994b) 'Parents and professionals: future directions', in Broding, J. and Bjorck-Akesson, E. (eds) *Methodological Issues in Research in Augmentative and Alternative Communication.* Jonkoping: Jonkoping University Press.

Beck-Gernsheim, E. (1992) 'Everything for the child – for better or worse?', in Björnberg, U. (ed.) *European Parents in the 1990s.* London: Transaction Publishers.

Beckman, P. J. and Beckman-Boyes, G. (eds) (1993) *Deciphering the System: A Guide for Families of Young Children with Disabilities.* Cambridge, MA: Brookline.

Beckman, P. *et al.* (1996) 'Preparing professionals to work with families on Early Intervention teams', in Bricker, D. and Widerstrom, A. (eds) *Preparing Personnel to Work with Infants and Young Children and Their Families: A Team approach.* Baltimore, MD: Paul H. Brookes.

Beckman, P. J. *et al.* (1995) 'Family involvement in Early Intervention: the evolution of family-centred services', in Beckman, P. J., Robinson, C. C., Rosenberg, S. and Filer, J. (eds) *Early Intervention for Children and their Families: Providing Services from Birth to Three.* Baltimore, MD: Paul H. Brookes.

Bendor, S. J. (1990) 'Anxiety and isolation in siblings of pediatric cancer patients: the need for prevention', *Social Work in Health Care*, 14, 17–35.

Beresford, B. (1994) *Positively Parents: Caring for a Severely Disabled Child.* London: HMSO.

Beresford, B. (1995) *Expert Opinions: Families with Severely Disabled Children.* York: Social Policy Research Unit/Joseph Rowntree Foundation.

Beresford, B. (1996) *Positively Parents: Caring for a Severely Disabled Child.* London: Social Policy Research Unit/HMSO.

Bergen, D. (1994) *Assessment Methods for Infants and Toddlers: Transdisciplinary Team Approaches.* New York: Teachers College Press.

Bernstein, B. (1975) *Class, Codes and Control (Vol. 3).* London: Routledge and Kegan Paul.

Binkard, B., Goldberg, M. and Goldberg, P. F. (eds) (1987) *Brothers and Sisters Talk with PACER.* Minneapolis, MN: PACER Center, Inc.

Björnberg, U. (1992) 'Parenting in transition: an introduction and summary', in Björnberg, U. (ed.) *European Parents in the 1990s.* London: Transaction Publishers.

Blackstone, S. W. and Williams, M. B. (1994) 'Family involvement in the AAC intervention process: conceptual and methodological issues', in Broding, J. and Bjorck-Akesson, E. (eds) *Methodological Issues in Research in Augmentative and Alternative Communication.* Jonkoping: Jonkoping University Press.

Blair, M. (1994) 'Interviews with black families', in Cohen, R. and Hughes, M. (eds) *School's Out.* London: Family Service Unit and Barnardo's.

Bourne, J., Bridges, L. and Searle, C. (1994) *Outcast England.* London: Institute of Race Relations.

Bourne, J. and McPake, J. (1991) *Partnership Teaching.* London: HMSO.

Bowlby, J. (1960) 'Grief and mourning in infancy and early childhood', *Psychoanalytic Study of the Child*, 15, 9–52.

Boyd, J. (1989) *Equality Issues in Primary Schools.* London: Paul Chapman.

Bray, A. *et al.* (1995) 'Fathers of children with disabilities: some experiences and reflections', *New Zealand Journal of Disability Studies*, 1 (1), 164–76.

Bredekamp, S. (1987) *Developmentally Appropriate Practice in Early Childhood Programmes Serving Children from Birth through Age Eight.* Washington DC: National Association for the Education of Young Children.

Brewer, G.A.D. and Kakalik, J. S. (1979) *Handicapped Children: Strategies for Improving Services.* New York: McGraw-Hill.

Brindlecombe, F. and Russell, P. (1988) *Honeylands: Developing a Service for Families with Handicapped Children.* London: National Children's Bureau.

Brinker, R. P. (1992) 'Family involvement in early intervention: accepting the unchangeable, changing the changeable and knowing the difference', *Topics in Early Childhood Special Education*, 12 (3), 307–32.

Bronfenbrenner, U. (1979) *The Ecology of Human Development: Experiments by Nature and Design.* Cambridge, MA: Harvard University Press.

Bronfenbrenner, U. (1990), in McMillan, B.(1990) 'Ecological Perspectives on individual human development', *Early Childhood Development*, 55, 33–42.

Brown, C. (1994a) 'Parents and professionals: future directions', in K. Ballard, (ed.) *Disability, Family, Whānau and Society.* Palmerston North, NZ: Dunmore Press.

Brown, C. (1994b) 'Special Education Policies of the 4th Labour Government, 1984–1990: An Interpretive Analysis', unpublished thesis, Massey University, Palmerston North, New Zealand.

Buckley, S. (1994) 'Early Intervention: the state of the art', in Carpenter, B. (ed.) *Early Intervention: Where Are We Now?* Oxford: Westminster Press.

Buckley, S. and Bird, G. (1995) 'Early intervention: how to help your child in the preschool years', *Down's Syndrome Trust Newsletter*, 5 (1), 1–5.

Byrne, E. A. and Cunningham, C. C. (1988) 'The effects of mentally handicapped children on families: a conceptual review', *Journal of Child Psychology and Psychiatry*, 26, 847–64.

Byrne, E. A., Cunningham, C. and Sloper, P. (1986) *Families and their Children with Down's Syndrome: One Feature in Common*, London: Routledge.

Cairns, N. *et al.* (1979) 'Malignancy', *Journal of Pediatrics*, 95, 484–7.

Cameron, R. (1986a) 'Research and evaluation: how effective is Portage?', in Cameron, R. J. (ed.) *Portage – Pre-schoolers, Parents and Professionals: Ten Years of Achievement*. Windsor: NFER–Nelson.

Cameron, R. (1986b) *Portage: The Years of Achievement*. Windsor: NFER–Nelson.

Campbell, P., Strickland, B. and La Forme, C. (1992) 'Enhancing parent participation in the individual family service plan', *Topics in Early Childhood Special Education*, 11 (4), 112–24.

Campion, J. (1992) *Working with Vulnerable Young Children: Early Intervention*. London: Cassell.

Carpenter, B. (ed.) (1994) *Early Intervention: Where Are We Now?* Oxford: Westminster College.

Carpenter, B. (1995a) 'Across the lifespan: educational opportunities for children with profound and multiple learning difficulties', *Early Child Development and Care*, 109, 75–82.

Carpenter, B. (1995b) 'Involving fathers: a preliminary evaluation of the IF project' (occasional paper). Oxford: Westminster College.

Carpenter, B. (1995c) 'Building an inclusive curriculum', in Ashcroft, K. and Palacio, D. (eds) *The Primary Teacher's Guide to the New National Curriculum*. London: Falmer.

Carpenter, B. (1995d) '"Tell me about Katie": attitudes of mainstream 7–8-year-olds to a peer with Down's syndrome', *Down's Syndrome: Research and Practice*, 3 (2), 45–52.

Carpenter, B. (1996a) 'Defining the family: towards a critical framework', paper presented to the First Education Colloquium (Helios II Programme), Luxembourg.

Carpenter, B. (1996b) 'Enabling partnership: families and schools', in Carpenter, B., Ashdown, R. and Bovair, K. (eds) *Enabling Access: Effective Teaching and Learning for Pupils with Learning Difficulties*. London: David Fulton.

Carpenter, B. and Carpenter, S. A. (1989) 'The Blythe Home–Liaison Playgroup: an early intervention scheme for very young children with special educational needs and their families', *Early Child Development and Care*, 5, 13–21.

Carpenter, B. and Herbert, E. (1994a) 'The peripheral parent: research issues and reflections on the role of fathers in early intervention', *PMLD Link*, 19 (Summer), 16–25.

Carpenter, B. and Herbert, E. (1994b) 'School–based support', in Mittler, P. and Mittler, H. (eds) *Innovations in Family Support for People with Learning Difficulties*. Chorley: Lisieux Hall.

Carpenter, B. and Herbert, E. (1994c) 'Fathers: the secondary partners', in Carpenter, B. (ed.) *Early Intervention: Where Are We Now?* Oxford: Westminster College.

Carpenter, B. and Herbert, E. (1995a) 'Including fathers: parent–professional considerations of the role of father in early intervention', *Network*, 4 (4), 4–11.

Carpenter, B. and Herbert, E. (1995b) 'Fathers: are early intervention strategies meeting their needs?' paper presented to the International Special Education Congress, Birmingham, UK.

Carpenter, B., Ashdown, R. and Bovair, K. (eds) (1996) *Enabling Access: Effective Teaching and Learning for Pupils with Learning Difficulties*. London: David Fulton.

Carr, W. and Kemmis, S. (1986) *Becoming Critical*, London: Falmer Press.

Carter, H. (1994) 'The territorial significance of language (Arwyddocad tiriogaethol iaith)', in Williams, R. H., Williams, H. and Davies, E. (eds) *Social Work and the Welsh Language – Gwaith Cymdeithasol a'r Iaith Gymraeg*. Cardiff: CCETSW Cymru.

Chaudhury, A. (1988) 'How special is special? The concerns of Bangladeshi parents', *Issues*, (Spring). London: Advisory Centre for Education.

Chodorow, N. (1990) 'Gender, relation, and difference in psychoanalytic perspectives', in Zanardi, C. (ed.) *Essential Papers on the Psychology of Women*. New York: New York University Press.

Clarkson, J. E. *et al.* (1996) 'Fathers of children with disabilities comment on health services', *New Zealand Medical Journal*, 109, 274–6.

Clements, J. C. *et al.* (1980) 'A home advisory service for pre-school children with developmental delays', *Child: Care, Health and Development*, **6** (1), 25–33.

Cleveland, D. W. and Miller, N. (1977) 'Attitudes and life commitments of older siblings of mentally retarded adults: an exploratory study', *Mental Retardation*, **15**, 38-41.

Cochran, M. (1990) 'Personal social networks as a focus of support', *Prevention in Human Services*, **9** (1), 45–67.

Coleman, S. V. (1990) 'The sibling of the retarded child: self-concept, deficit compensation motivation, and perceived parental behavior', *Dissertation Abstracts International*, **51** (10-B), 5023.

Cotton, E. (1984) 'Integration of disciplines in the treatment and education of children with cerebral palsy', in Levitt, S.(ed.) *Paediatric Developmental Theory.* Oxford: Blackwell Scientific Publications.

Council of Europe (1991) *Community and Ethnic Relations in Europe (MG-CR(91)1).* Strasbourg: Council of Europe.

CRE (1992) *Second Review of the Race Relations Act, 1976.* London: CRE.

CRE (1996) *Special Educational Need Assessment in Strathclyde.* London: CRE.

Cullberg, J. (1975) *Kris och Utveckling.* Stockholm: Natur och Kultur.

Cummins, J. (1984) *Bilingualism and Special Education.* Avon: Multilingual Matters.

Cunningham, C. (1994) 'Telling parents their child has a disability', in Mittler, P. and Mittler, H. (eds) *Innovations in Family Support for People with Learning Difficulties.* Chorley: Lisieux Hall.

Cunningham, C. C. and Davis, H. (1985) *Working with Parents: Frameworks for Collaboration.* Milton Keynes: Open University Press.

Curnyn, J. *et al.* (1990) 'Special educational need and ethnic minority children', *Professional Development Initiatives 1989–90* (Edinburgh: Scottish Office Education Department), 271–300.

Dale, N. (1996) *Working with Families of Children with Special Needs: Partnership and Practice.* London: Routledge.

David, M. (1993) *Parents, Gender and Educational Reform.* Cambridge: Polity Press.

David, T. (1996) 'Their right to play', in Nutbrown, C. (ed.) *Respectful Educators, Capable Learners: Children's Rights and Early Educators.* London: Paul Chapman.

Dempsey, I. (1993) 'The measurement of parental empowerment', in Arthur, M., Conway, R. and Foreman, P. (eds) *Quality and Equality in Intellectual Disability.* Newcastle, NSW: ASSID.

DES (1978) *Special Educational Needs: The Report of the Committee of Enquiry into the Education of Handicapped Children and Young People (The Warnock Report).* London: HMSO.

DES (1990) *Starting with Quality (Rumbold Report).* London: HMSO.

Detheridge, T. and Detheridge, M. (1997) *Literacy through Symbols.* London: David Fulton.

de Vaus, D. (1994) *Letting Go: Relationships between Adults and their Parents.* Melbourne: Oxford University Press.

DfE (1994) *Education Act 1993: Code of Practice on the Identification and Assessment of Special Educational Needs.* London: HMSO.

DfEE (1996a) *Work and Family: Ideas and Options for Childcare.* London: DfEE.

DfEE (1996b) *Nursery Education Scheme: The Next Steps.* London: DfEE.

DHSS (1976) *Fit for the Future: The Report of the Committee on Child Health Services (Court Report).* London: HMSO.

Diniz, F. A. and Pal, D. (1997) *Ethnic Minority Parents and Special Education Provision.* Edinburgh: Moray House Institute of Education.

Dixon, N. and Flanagan, R. (1984) *Meeting the Social Work Needs of Families with Mentally Handicapped Children* (Anson House Pre-school Project Papers 4). London: Barnardo's.

DoH (1991) *The Children Act 1989: Guidance and Regulations (Vols 1–9).* London: HMSO.

Doherty, J. (1992) 'A sibling remembers', *Candlelighters Childhood Cancer Foundation Quarterly Newsletter.* **16**, 4–6.

Dunst, C. (1985) 'Rethinking Early Intervention', *Analysis and Intervention in Developmental Disabilities*, **5**, 165–201.

Dunst, C. J. (1990) 'Family support principles: checklists for program builders', *Family Systems Intervention Monograph Series*, **2** (5).

Dunst, C. J., Trivette, C. M. and Deal, A. (1988) *Enabling and Empowering Families: Principles and Guidelines for Practice.* Cambridge, MA: Brookline.

Elkind, D. (1986) 'Formal education and early childhood education: an essential difference,' *Phi Delta Kappan*, **67**, 631–6.

Elkind, D. (1987) *Miseducation Preschoolers at Risk*. Boston: Allyn and Bacon.

Eurostats (1996) *Demographic Statistics 1996*. Luxembourg: Eurostat Press Office.

Faber, A. and Mazlish, E. (1988) *Siblings without Rivalry: How to Help your Children Live together so You Can Live too*. New York: Avon.

Faber, A. and Mazlish, E. (1991) *How To Talk so Kids Will Listen and Listen so Kids Will Talk*. New York: Avon.

Farber, B. (1960) 'Family organization and crisis: maintenance of integration in families with a severely mentally retarded child', *Monographs of the Society for Research in Child Development*, **25** (1, Serial No. 75).

Ferguson, P. M. and Ferguson, D. (1987) 'Parents and professionals', in Knoblock, P. (ed.) *Understanding Exceptional Children and Youth*. Boston, MA: Little, Brown.

Ferguson, D. and Meyer, G. (1991) *Ecological Assessment*. Oregon: University of Oregon (Schools Project).

Ferri, E. and Saunders, A. (1991) *Parents, Professionals, and Pre-school Centres: A Study of Barnardo's Provision*. London: Barnardo's.

Fewell, R. (1986) 'A handicapped child in the family', in Fewell, R. and Vadasy, P. (eds) *Families of Handicapped Children*. Austin, Tx: Pro-Ed.

Fish, T. (Producer) (1993) *The Next Step* [Videotape], Columbus, OH: Publications Office, Nissonger Center UAP, Ohio State University. Available from T. Fish, The Nisonger Center, Ohio State University, 1580 Canon Dr. Columbus, Ohio, 43210, USA.

Fish, T. and Fitzgerald, G. M. (1980) 'A transdisciplinary approach to working with adolescent siblings of the mentally retarded: a group experience', paper presented to Social Work with Groups Symposium, Arlington, Texas. Available as above.

Fitton, P. (1994) *Listen to Me: Communicating the Needs of People with Profound Intellectual and Multiple Disabilities*. London: Jessica Kingsley.

Foley, G. M. (1990) 'Portrait of the arena evaluation: assessment in the transdisciplinary approach', in Gibbs, E. D. and Teti, D. M. (eds) *Interdisciplinary Assessment of Infants: A Guide for Early Intervention Professionals*. Baltimore, MD: Paul H. Brookes.

Ford, G. (1991) *Report of the Committee of Inquiry into Racism and Xenophobia*. Luxembourg: Office of the European Communities.

Fowle, C. (1973) 'The effect of a severely mentally retarded child on his family', *American Journal of Mental Deficiency*, **73**, 468–73.

Fyffe, C. (1995) 'Reflections on service co-ordination: why is it more complex than it seems?', paper prepared for the Victorian Early Intervention Association 11th Annual Conference, Melbourne, Australia.

Gabba, M. (1994) 'Some things are unacceptable', *Special Children*, February, 19–20.

Gabel, H. and Kotsch, L. (1981) 'Extended families and young handicapped children', *Topics in Early Childhood Special Education*, **1**, 29–35.

Gallimore, R. *et al.* (1989) 'The social construction of ecocultural niches', *Journal of Mental Retardation*, **94**, 216–30.

Garbarino, J. (1990) 'The human ecology of human risk', in Meisels, S. J. and Shonkoff, J. P. (eds) *Handbook of Early Childhood Intervention*. Cambridge: Cambridge University Press.

Gardner, C. (1996) 'A grandparent's perspective: a special relationship', in Schalock, R. and Siperstein, G. (eds) *Quality of Life (Vol. 1): Conceptualization and Measurement*. Washington, DC: American Association on Mental Retardation.

Gath, A. (1974) 'Sibling reactions to mental handicap: a comparison of the brothers and sisters of mongol children', *Journal of Child Psychology and Psychiatry*, **15**, 187–98.

Gecas, V. (1979) 'The influence of social class on socialization', in Burr, W. R., Hill, R., Nye, F. J. and Reiss, I. L. (eds.) *Contemporary Theories about the Family (Vol. 1)*. New York: The Free Press.

George, J. (1988) 'Therapeutic intervention for grandparents and extended family of children with developmental delays', *Mental Retardation*, **26**, 369–75.

Giddens, A. (1991) *Modernity and Self-Identity: Self and Society in the Late Modern Age*. Cambridge: Polity/Blackwell.

Gillborn, D. and Gipps, C. (1996) *Recent Research on the Achievements of Ethnic Minority Pupils* (OFSTED Reviews of Research). London: HMSO.

Goffman, E. (1963) *Stigma*. New York: Simon and Schuster.

Goldschmied, E. and Jackson, S. (1994) *People under Three: Young Children in Day Care.* London: Routledge.

Goldschmied, E. and Selleck, D. (1996) *Commuinication between Babies in their First Year.* London: National Children's Bureau.

Grossman, F. (1972) *Brothers and Sisters of Retarded Children: An Exploratory Study.* Syracuse, NY: Syracuse University Press.

Guralnick, M. J. (1991) 'The next decade of research on the effectiveness of early intervention', *Exceptional Children*, **58** (2), 174–83.

Gustavsson, A. (1989) *Samhällsideal och Föräldraansvar: Om Föräldrar till Förståndshandikappade Barn.* Stockholm: Almqvist and Wiksell.

Hall, D. (1995) *Assessing the Needs of Bilingual Pupils.* London: David Fulton.

Hallahan, D. P., Kauffman, J. M. and Wills Lloyd, J. (1996) *Introduction to Learning Disabilities.* London: Allyn and Bacon.

Hallden, G. (1992) *Föräldrars Tankar om Barn: Uppfostringsideologi som Kultur.* Stockholm: Carlssons Bokförlag.

Hautamäki, A. (1982) *Social Class, Activity, Environment and Voluntary Learning: An Interpretation and Application of Vygotsky's Concepts.* North Carelia: University of Joensuu.

Hautamäki, A. (1995) *Masochism – The Riddle of Femininity? A Developmental Perspective.* Helsinki: University of Helsinki, Swedish School of Social Science.

Hautamäki, A. (1996) *Stress and Stressors in Parenting a Developmentally Delayed Child at Different Life Stages: A Cross-Sectional Nordic Study with a Representative Sample of Nonhandicapped Children* (Research Report No. 165). Helsinki: University of Helsinki.

Hautamäki, A. (1997) 'The post-modern family – the interaction between the home and the school', in Jakku-Sihvonen, R. (ed.) *Evaluating the Quality of Teaching and Learning.* Helsinki: Finnish Board of Education.

Hearn, B. (1996) *Child Support and Protection: A Practical Approach.* London: National Children's Bureau.

Hebden, J. (1985) *She'll Never Do Anything, Dear.* London: Souvenir Press.

Herbert, E. (1994) 'Becoming a special family', in David, T. (ed.) *Working Together for Young Children.* London: Routledge.

Herbert, E. and Carpenter, B. (1994) 'Fathers – the secondary partners: professional perceptions and a father's reflections', *Children and Society*, **8** (1), 31–41.

Herbert, E. and Moir, J. (1996) 'Children with special educational needs – a collaborative and inclusive style of working', in Nutbrown, C. (ed.) *Respectful Educators, Capable Learners: Children's Rights and Early Educators.* London: Paul Chapman.

Home Office (1997) *Preventing Children Offending: A Consultation Document.* London: Home Office.

Hornby, G. (1989) 'Launching parent-to-parent schemes', *British Journal of Special Education.* **15** (2), 77–8.

Hornby, G. (1991) 'Parental involvement', in Mitchell, D. and Brown, R. I. (eds) *Early Intervention Studies for Young Children with Special Needs.* Norwich: Chapman Hall.

Hornby, G. (1995) *Working with Parents of Children with Special Needs.* London: Cassell.

Hornby, G. and Ashworth, T. (1994) 'Grandparents' support for families who have children with disabilities', *Journal of Child and Family Studies*, **3**, 403–12.

Husbands, L. (1996) 'Working with pre-school children with PMLD and their families: a personal view', *PMLD–Link*, **24**, 2–3.

Irving, B. (1997) 'Parental participation: essential partners in guidance', *Pastoral Care*, **15** (1), 6–9.

Johnson, C. and Crowder, J. (1994) *Autism: From Tragedy to Triumph.* Boston, MA: Branden Publishers.

Johnson-Martin, N. M. *et al.* (1990) *The Carolina Curriculum for Infants and Toddlers with Special Needs* (2nd edn). Baltimore, MD: Paul H. Brookes.

Jones, E. J. (1994) 'A study of parental perception and evaluation of the South Glamorgan Home Advisory Service' (unpublished). Cardiff: University of Cardiff.

Jones, E. J. (forthcoming) *The Types of Early Intervention Available in South Glamorgan; and Parental Accounts of their Children's Experience of Service Provision* (Ph. D. thesis). Cardiff: University of Cardiff.

Jowett, S. and Baginsky, M., with MacNeil, M. M. (1991) *Building Bridges: Parental Involvement in Schools.* Windsor: NFER–Nelson.

Jupp, S. (1992) *Making the Right Start: A Practical Guide to Help Break the News to Families when their Baby has been Born with a Disability.* Hyde: Open Eyed Publications.

Kazak, A. and Marvin, R. (1984) 'Differences, difficulties and adaptation: stress and social networks in families with a handicapped child', *Family Relations*, 33, 67–77.

Kelly, G. (1955) *The Psychology of Personal Constructs.* New York: Norton.

Kessen, W. (1979) 'The American child and other cultural inventions', *American Psychologist*, 34 (10), 815–20.

Kivnick, K. (1983) 'Dimensions of grandparent meaning: deductive conceptualization and empirical derivation', *Journal of Personality and Social Psychology*, 44, 1056–68.

Koch-Hattem, A. (1986) 'Siblings' experience of pediatric cancer: interviews with children', *Health and Social Work*, 10, 107–17.

Köhler, L. (ed.) (1990) *Barn och Barnfamiljer i Norden: En studie av Välfärd, Hälsa och Livskvalitet – Resultatdelen.* Gothenburg: Nordiska hälsovårDshögskolan.

Kollberg, E., Hautamäki, A. and Heiberg, A. (eds) (1997*) Barn med Downs Syndrom.* Stockholm: Natur och Kultur.

Lacey, P. and Lomas, J. (1993) *Support Services and the Curriculum: A Practical Guide to Collaboration.* London: David Fulton.

Landerholm, E. (1990) 'The transdisciplinary team', *Teaching Exceptional Children*, (Winter).

Leder, J. M. (1991) *Brothers and Sisters: How They Shape our Lives.* New York: St. Martin's Press.

Levy, J. M. *et al.* (1996) 'The support network of mothers of younger and adult children with mental retardation and developmental disabilities receiving care management', *British Journal of Developmental Disabilities*, 42 (82), 24–31.

Lewis, A. (1995) *Children's Understanding of Disability.* London: Routledge.

Lobato, D. J. (1990) *Brothers, Sisters, and Special Needs: Information and Activities for Helping Young Siblings of Children with Chronic Illnesses and Developmental Disabilities.* Baltimore, MD: Paul H. Brookes.

Lobato, D. *et al.* (1987) 'Psychosocial characteristics of pre-school siblings of handicapped and nonhandicapped children', *Journal of Abnormal Child Psychology*, 15, 329–38.

MacWilliam, P. J. and Bailey, D. B. (1993) *Working Together with Children and Families: Case Studies in Early Intervention.* Baltimore, MD: Paul H. Brookes.

Mäki, I. (1994) 'Ecological approach and early intervention', in Leskinen, M. (ed.) *Family in Focus.* Jyväskylä: Jyväskylä University Press.

Manuel, P. (1996) 'A parent's perspective', paper presented to the National Children's Bureau Conference, London.

Marfo, K. and Dinero, T. (1991) 'Assessing early intervention outcomes: beyond program variables', *International Journal of Disability, Development and Education*, 38 (3), 289–303.

Marfo, K. and Kysela, G. M. (1985) 'Early intervention with mentally handicapped children: a critical appraisal of applied research', *Journal of Paediatric Psychology*, 10 (3), 305.

Marks, N. and McLanahan, S. (1993) 'Gender, family structure, and social support among parents', *Journal of Marriage and Family*, 55, 481–493.

Mattus, M. R. (1994) 'Interview as intervention: strategies to empower families of children with disabilities', in Leskinen, M. (ed.) *Family in Focus.* Jyväskylä: Jyväskylä University Press.

McBride, S. L. *et al.* (1993) 'Implementation of family-centred services: perceptions of families and professionals', *Journal of Early Intervention*, 17 (4), 414–30.

McConachie, H. (1986) *Parents and Young Mentally Handicapped Children: A Review of Research Issues.* London: Croom Helm.

McConachie, H. (1994) 'Implications of a model of stress and coping for services to families of young disabled children', *Child: Care, Health and Development*, 20, 1–10.

McConkey, R. (1994) 'Early Intervention: planning futures, shaping years', *Mental Handicap Research*, 7 (1), 4–15.

McCullough, M. E. (1981) 'Parent and sibling definition of situation regarding transgenerational shift in care of a handicapped child', *Dissertation Abstracts International*, 42 (1-B), 161.

McEwen, M. (1995) *Tackling Racism in Europe.* Oxford: Berg.

McGonigel, M. J., Kaufmann, R. K. and Johnson, B. H. (1991) 'A family-centred process for the individualised family service plan', *Journal of Early Intervention*, 15 (1), 46–56.

McKinley, I. (1994) 'Disclosure of developmental disorders', paper presented to the international seminar on 'Partnership between Parents and Professionals in the Care of Children and Young People with Learning Disabilities', UMIST, Manchester.

Mental Health Foundation (1997) *Don't Forget Us: Children with Learning Disabilities and Severe Challenging Behaviour (Report of Committee, Mental Health Foundation)*. London: HMSO.

Meyer, D. (1986) *The Father Role: Applied Perspectives*, New York: John Cowley.

Meyer, D. (1993) 'Lessons learned: cognitive coping strategies of overlooked family members', in Turnbull, A., Patterson, J., Behr, S., Murphy, D., Marquis, J. and Blue-Banning, M. (eds) *Cognitive Coping, Families and Disability*. Baltimore, MD: Paul H. Brookes.

Meyer, D. (1995) *Uncommon Fathers: Reflections on Raising a Child with a Disability*. Bethesda, MD: Woodbine House.

Meyer, D. and Vadasy, P. (1986) *Grandparent Workshops: How to Organize Workshops for Grandparents of Children with Handicaps*. Seattle, DC: University of Washington Press.

Meyer, D. J. and Vadasy, P. F. (1994) *Sibshops: Workshops for Siblings of Children with Special Needs* (2nd edn). Baltimore, MD: Paul H. Brookes.

Mirfin-Veitch, B., Bray, A. and Watson, M. (1996) '"They really do care": grandparents as informal support sources for parents of children with disabilities', *New Zealand Journal of Disability Studies*, **2**, 136–48.

Mirfin-Veitch, B., Bray, A. and Watson, M. (1997) '"We're just that sort of family": intergenerational relationships in families of children with disabilities', *Family Rel;ations*, **46** (3).

Mittler, P. (1994) 'Early intervention: which way forward?', in Carpenter, B. (ed.) *Early Intervention: Where Are We Now?* Oxford: Westminster College.

Mittler, P. (1996) 'Laying the foundations for self-advocacy: the role of home and school', in Coupe O'Kane, J. and Goldbart, J. (eds) *Whose Choice? Contentious Issues for those Working with People with Learning Difficulties*, London: David Fulton.

Moore, T. G. (1990) 'Helping young children with developmental problems: an overview of current early intervention aims and practices', *Australian Journal of Early Childhood*, **15**, 3.

Morrow, J. (1992) 'Terry Cunningham: a brother who sticks up for his siblings', *Parents and Friends Together for People with Deaf-Blindness News*, **1** (5), 2.

Moyles, J. (1994) *The Excellence of Play*. Milton Keynes: Open University Press.

Murphy, A. T. (1979) Members of the family: sisters and brothers of handicapped children, *Volta Review*, **81**, 352–62.

Murray, G. and Jampolsky, G. G. (eds) (1982) *Straight from the Siblings: Another Look at the Rainbow*. Berkeley, CA: Celestial Arts.

Nester, J. (1989) 'Adult sibling panel notes', *Down Syndrome Association of New Jersey Newsletter*, March.

Newson, E. and Davies, J. (1994) 'Supporting the siblings of children with autism and related developmental disorders', in Mittler, P. and Mittler, H. (1995) *Innovations in Family Support for People with Learning Disabilities*. Chorley: Lisieux Hall.

Nihira, K., Weisner, T. and Bernheimer, L. P. (1994) 'Ecocultural assessment in families of children with developmental delays: construct and concurrent validities', *American Journal on Mental Retardation*, **98** (5), 551–6.

Noonan, M. J. and McCormick, L. (1993) *Early Intervention in Natural Environments: Methods and Procedures*. California: Brooks/Cole.

OECD (1987) *Immigrant Children at School*. Paris: Centre for Educational Research and Innovation.

OFSTED (1993) *First Class: The Standards and Quality of Education in Reception Classes*. London: HMSO.

OFSTED (1995) *The OFSTED Handbook: Guidance on the Inspection of Special Schools*. London: HMSO.

Oppenheim, A. N. (1992) *Questionnaire Design, Interviewing and Attitude Measurement*. London: New Edition Printer.

Parfit, J. (1975) 'Siblings of handicapped children', *Special Education: Forward Trends*, **2**, 19–21.

Patton, M. Q. (1983) *Qualitative Evaluation Methods*. London: SAGE.

Peterander, F. (1995) *Early Intervention: Research Report to the Helios II Programme*. Munich: Ludwig-Maximilian University.

Pieterse, M., Bochner, S. and Bettison, S. (eds) (1988) *Early Intervention for Children with Disabilities: The Australian Experience*. NSW: Macquarie University.

Podeanu-Czehotsky, I. (1975) 'Is it only the child's guilt? Some aspects of family life of cerebral palsied children', *Rehabilitation Literature*, **36**, 308–11.

Powell, T. H. and Gallagher, P. A. (1993) *Brothers and Sisters: A Special Part of Exceptional Families* (2nd edn). Baltimore, MD: Paul H. Brookes.

Pugh, G. (1994) 'The sooner, the better: early education', paper presented to the 'Our Children, Our Future' Conference, Primary Schools Research and Development Group, University of Birmingham.

Quine, L. and Pahl, J. (1991) 'Stress and coping in mothers caring for a child with severe learning difficulties: a test of Lazarus' transaction model of coping', *Journal of Community and Applied Social Psychology*, **1** (1), 57–70.

Ranger, T., Samad, Y. and Stuart, O. (eds) *Culture, Identity and Politics: Ethnic Minorities in Britain.* Aldershot: Avebury.

Rapoport, R. N. (1970) 'Three dilemmas in action research', *Human Relations*, **23**, 499–513.

Redding, D. (1990) 'Suffering in silence', *Community Care*, **842** (29), 17–19.

Rehal, A. (1989) 'Involving Asian parents in the statementing procedure – the way forward', *Educational Psychology in Practice*, **4**, 189–92.

Remsberg, B. (1989) *What It Means to Have a Handicapped Brother or Sister* (unpublished manuscript).

Revill, S. and Blunden, R. (1979) 'A home training service for pre-school developmentally delayed children', *Behaviour Research and Therapy*, **17**, 207–14.

Reynolds, D. (1995) 'Creating an educational system of Wales', *Welsh Journal of Education*, **4** (2), 4–21.

Robson, C. (1993) *Real World Research: A Resource for Social Scientists and Practitioner-Researchers.* Oxford: Blackwell.

Rodrigue, J. R., Morgan, S. B. and Geffken, G. R. (1992) 'Psychological adaptation of fathers of children with autism, Down's syndrome and normal development', *Journal of Autism and Developmental Disorders*, **22** (2), 249–63.

Roll, J. (1991) *What is a Family?* London: FPSC.

Russell, P. (1994) 'Surveillance and intervention: special issues in child care services', in Carpenter, B. (ed.) *Early Intervention: Where Are We Now?* Oxford: Westminster College.

Russell, P. (1996) *The Role of the Named Person.* London: Council for Disabled Children.

Russell, P. (1997) 'Parents as partners: some early impressions of the implementation of the Code of Practice', in Wolfendale, S. (ed.) *Working with Parents of SEN Children after the Code of Practice.* London: David Fulton.

Sameroff, A. J. and Fiese, B. H. (1990) 'Transactional regulation and early intervention', in Meisels, S. J. and Shonkoff, J. P. (eds) *Handbook of Early Childhood Intervention.* Cambridge: Cambridge University Press.

Sandler, A., Warren, S. and Raver, S. (1995) 'Grandparents as a source of support for parents of children with disabilities: a brief report', *Mental Retardation*, **3**, 248–9.

SCAA (1996) *Desirable Outcomes for Children's Learning on Entering Compulsory Education.* London: DfEE/SCAA.

Schell, G. (1981) 'The young handicapped child', *Topics in Early Childhood Special Education*, **1**, 21–7.

Schild, S. (1976) 'Counselling with parents of retarded children living at home', in Turner, F. J. (ed.) *Differential Diagnosis and Treatment in Social Work.* New York: The Free Press.

Schofield, J. (1991) 'Practical standards,' *Nursing Times*, **86** (8), 31–32.

Schorr-Ribera, H. (1992) 'Caring for siblings during diagnosis and treatment', *Candlelighters Childhood Cancer Foundation Quarterly Newsletter*, **16**, 1–3.

Schweinhart, L. J. and Weikart, D. P. (1993) *A Summary of Significant Benefits: The High/Scope Perry Preschool Study through Age 27.* Ypsilanti, MI: High/Scope Foundation.

Seligman, M. (1979) *Strategies for Helping Parents of Exceptional Children.* New York: The Free Press.

Seligman, M. (1991) 'Grandparents of disabled grandchildren: hopes, fears, and adaptation', *Families in Society*, **24,** 147–52.

Seligman, M. and Darling, R. (1989) *Ordinary Families, Special Children.* New York: The Guilford Press.

Shah, R. (1992) *The Silent Minority: Children with Disabilities in Asian Families.* London: National Children's Bureau.

Shearer, M. S. and Shearer, D. E. (1972) 'The Portage Project: model for early childhood education', *Exceptional Children*, **39** (3), 210–17.

Shelley, P. (1996) 'Supporting siblings of children with special needs', paper presented to the Network of Parents of Children with Special Needs and Contact a Family Workshop, July.

Shonkoff, J. P. and Meisels, S. J. (1990) 'Early childhood intervention: the evolution of a concept', in Meisels, S. J. and Shonkoff, J. P. (eds) *Handbook of Early Childhood Intervention.* Cambridge, MA: Harvard University Press.

Shonkoff, J. P. *et al.* (1992) 'Development of infants with disabilities and their families: implications for theory and service delivery with commentary by Sameroff, A. J.', *Monographs of the Society for Research in Child Development,* **57** (6).

Shorrocks, D. (1992) 'Evaluating key stage 1 assessments: the testing time of May 1991', *Early Years,* **13** (1), 16–20.

Shotter, J. (1993) *Cultural Politics of Everyday Life,* Milton Keynes.: Open University Press.

Simeonsson, R. J. and Bailey, D. B. (1990) 'Family dimensions in early intervention', in Meisels, S. J. and Shonkoff, J. P. (eds) *Handbook of Early Childhood Intervention.* Cambridge: Cambridge University Press.

Simons, R. (1985) *After the Tears: Parents talk about Raising a Child with a Disability.* Orlando, FL: Harcourt Brace Javanovich.

Siraj-Blatchford, I. (1994) *The Early Years: Laying the Foundations for Racial Equality.* Stoke-on-Trent: Trentham.

Skutnabb-Kangas, T. and Cummins, J. (eds) (1988) *Minority Education.* Avon: Multilingual Matters.

Sloper, P. *et al.* (1991) 'Factors related to stress and satisfaction with life in families of children with Down's syndrome', *Journal of Child Psychology and Psychiatry,* **32** (4), 655–76.

Smith, A. *et al.* (1995) 'Caring for the caregivers: how does it influence caring for the children?', paper presented to the Early Childhood Convention, Auckland, New Zealand.

Smith, J., Keen, P. and Daley, F. (1996) 'PRESAM: a pre-school assessment model', *Educational Psychology in Practice,* **12** (1), 3–9.

Solnit, A. J. and Stark, M. H. (1961) 'Mourning and the birth of a defective child', *Psychoanalytic Study of the Child,* **16,** 523–37.

Sonnek, I. (1986) 'Grandparents and the extended family of handicapped children', in Fewell, R. and Vadasy, P. (eds) *Families of Handicapped Children.* Austin, Tx: Pro-Ed.

Sourkes, B. (1990) 'Siblings count too', *Candlelighters Childhood Cancer Foundation Youth Newsletter,* **12** (2), 6.

Stenhouse, L. (1975) *An Introduction to Curriculum Research and Development.* London: Heinemann.

Stoneman, Z. (1989) 'Comparison groups in research on families with mentally retarded members: a methodological and conceptual review', *American Journal on Mental Retardation,* **94**(3), 195–215.

Stoneman, Z. and Brody, G. (1993) 'Sibling relationships in the family context', in Stoneman, Z. and Berman, P. (eds) *The Effects of Mental Retardation, Disability, and Illness on Sibling Relationships,* Baltimore, MD: Paul H. Brookes.

Stoneman, Z. *et al.* (1987) 'Mentally retarded children and their older same-sex siblings: naturalistic in-home observations', *American Journal of Mental Retardation,* **92,** 290–8.

Stoneman, Z. *et al.* (1988) 'Child care responsibilities, peer relations, and sibling conflict: older siblings of mentally retarded children,' *American Journal of Mental Retardation,* **93,** 174–83.

Stoneman, Z. *et al.* (1989) 'Role relations between mentally retarded children and their older siblings: observations in three in-home contexts,' *Research in Developmental Disabilities,* **10,** 61–76.

Strauss, A. and Corbin, J. (1990) *Basics of Qualitative Research.* London: Sage.

Sturmey, P. and Crisp, A. (1986) 'Portage guide to early education: a review of research', *Educational Psychology,* **6** (2), 139–54.

Sylva, K. (1996) *Evaluation of the High/Scope Programme.* Oxford: Oxford University Press.

Talay-Ongan, A. (1991) 'A comprehensive transdisciplinary centre-based model of early intervention', *Early Child Development and Care,* **72,** 69–79.

Titterton, M. (1992) 'Managing threats to welfare: the search for a new paradigm of welfare', *Journal of Social Policy,* **21** (1), 1–23.

Tolston, A. (1977) *The Units of Masculinity.* London: Tavistock Publications.

Tomlinson, S. (1989) 'Asian pupils and special issues', *British Journal of Special Education,* **16** (3), 119–22.

Tomlinson, S. (1995) 'Ethnic minorities: involved partners or problem parents?', in Munn, P. (ed.)

186   *Families in Context*

Parents and Schools. London: Routledge.

Tönnies, F. (1887) *Gemeinschaft und Gesellschaft*. Leipzig: Abhandlung des Communismus und des Socialismus als empirischer Culturformen.

Trevarthen, C. (1992) 'An infant's motives for speaking and thinking in the culture', in Old, A. H. (ed.) *The Dialogical Alternative*. Oxford: Oxford University Press.

Troyna, B. (1993) *Racism and Education*. Buckingham: Open University.

Troyna, B. and Siraj-Blatchford, I. (1993) 'Providing support or denying access? The experiences of students designated ESL and SN in a multi-ethnic secondary school', *Educational Review*, **45** (1), 3–11.

Turnbull, A. and Turnbull, R. (1990) *Families, Professionals and Exceptionality: A Special Partnership* (2nd edn). Columbus: Merrill.

Turnbull, A. P. and Turnbull, H. R. (1993) 'Participatory research on cognitive coping: from concepts to research planning', in Turnbull, A. P., Patterson, J. M., Behr, S. K., Murphy, D. L., Marquis, J. G. and Blue-Banning, M. J. (eds) *Cognitive Coping, Families and Disability*, Baltimore, MD: Paul H. Brookes.

Turnbull, A. *et al.* (1986) 'Family research and intervention: a value and ethical examination', in Dokecki, P. and Zaner, R. (eds) *Ethics of Dealing with People with Severe Handicaps: Toward a Research Agenda*. Baltimore, MD: Paul H. Brookes.

Twiss, D. (Chair) (1989) *Report of the 'Before Five' Special Education Working Group, NZ Government Implementation Unit for 'Tomorrow's Schools'*. Wellington, NZ: NZ Government Implementation Unit.

Twiss, D., Stewart, B. and Corby, M. (1996) 'Early intervention services in NZ: Early beginnings, current provisions and challenges for future development'. Paper presented at the IASSID 10th Congress for Mental Retardation, Helsinki, 8–13 July 1996.

UN (1993) *The Standard Rules on the Equalization of Opportunities for Persons with Disabilities*. New York: UN.

United Nations Educational, Scientific and Cultural Organization (UNESCO)/Government of Spain (1994) *The Salamanca Statement and Framework for Action on Special Needs Education*. Geneva: UNESCO.

Utting, D. (1995) *Family and Parenthood: Supporting Families, Preventing Breakdown*. York: Rowntree Foundation.

Vadasy, P. (1987) 'Grandparents of children with special needs: supports especially for grandparents', *Children's Health Care*, **16**, 21–3.

Vadasy, P. and Fewell, R. (1986) 'Mothers of deaf-blind children', in Fewell, R. and Vadasy, P. (eds) *Families of Handicapped Children*. Austin, Tx: Pro-Ed.

Vadasy, P., Fewell, R. and Meyer, D. (1986) 'Grandparents of children with special needs: insights into their experiences and concerns', *Journal of the Division for Early Childhood*, **10**, 36–44.

Vincent, C. (1996) *Parents and Teachers*. London: Falmer.

Virpiranta-Sala, M. (1994) 'The development of parenthood in a family with an exceptional child', in Leskinen, M. (ed.) *Family in Focus*. Jyväskylä: Jyväskylä University Press.

Visser, J. and Upton, G. (1993) *Special Education in Britain after Warnock*. London: David Fulton.

Vygotsky, L. (1978) *Mind in Society: The Development of Upper Level Psychological Processes*. Cambridge, MA: Harvard University Press.

Waddington, L. *et al.* (1996) *How Can Disabled Persons in the EU Achieve Equal Rights as Citizens?* Brussels: Secretariat of European Day of Disabled Persons.

Waisbren, S. (1980) 'Parents reactions after the birth of a developmentally disabled child', *American Journal of Mental Deficiency*, **84**, 345–51.

Walker, M. (1985) *Makaton Vocabulary Development Project*. Camberley: Makaton Vocabulary Development Project. Available from MVDP, 31 Firwood Drive, Camberley, Surrey, UK, GU15 3QD.

Watson, J. (1991) 'The Queen', *Down Syndrome News*, **15** (8), 108.

Wehn, I. and Sommerschild, H. (1991) *Når Funksjonshemmede Barn Blir Ungdommer*, Tano: Institutt for Sosialmedisin og Barnepsykiatrisk Klinikk.

Weiser, T. S. and Gallimore, R. (1994) 'Ecocultural studies of families adapting to childhood developmental delays: unique features, defining differences and applied implications', in Leskinen, M. (ed.) *Family in Focus*. Jyväskylä: Jyväskylä University Press.

Welsh Office (1994) *The Welsh Mental Handicap Strategy: Guidance 1994*. Cardiff: Welsh Office.

Westra, M. (1992) 'An open letter to my parents', *Sibling Information Network Newsletter,* **8**(1), 4.

Whitebrook, M., Howes, C. and Phillips, D. (1990) *Who Cares? Childcare Teachers and the Quality of Care in America.* Oakland: Childcare Employee Project.

Wikler, L. (1984) 'Chronic stresses of families of mentally retarded children', in Henninger, M. L. and Nesselroad, E. M. (eds) *Working with Parents of Handicapped Children.* Lanham, MD: University Press of America.

Wikler, L., Wasow, M. and Hatfield, E. (1981) 'Chronic sorrow revisited: parent vs professional depiction of the adjustment of parents of mentally retarded children', *American Journal of Orthopsychiatry,* **51**, 63–70.

Wilcock, P. (1981) 'The Portage Project in South Glamorgan', in Pugh, G. (ed.) *Parents as Partners.* London: NCB.

Williams, M. (1995) 'Thoughts of the future', in Blackstone, S. and Pressman, H. (eds) *Outcomes in AAC.* Monterey, CA: Augmentative Communication Inc.

Wills, R. (1994) 'It is time to stop', in Ballard, K. (ed.) *Disability, Family, Whānau and Society.* Palmerston North, NZ: Dunmore Press.

Wilton, K. R. and Renaut, J. (1986) 'Stress levels in families with intellectually handicapped pre-school children and families with non-handicapped pre-school children', *Journal of Mental Deficiency Research,* **30**, 163–9.

Wolfendale, S. (1989) *Parental Involvement: Developing Networks between School, Home and Community.* London: Cassell.

Wolfendale, S. (1995) 'Parental Involvement', in Stobbs, P. (ed.) *Schools SEN Policy Pack.* London: National Children's Bureau.

Wright, L. S. (1976) 'Chronic grief: the anguish of being an exceptional parent', *The Exceptional Child,* **23**, 160–9.

Wyman, L. (1986) *Multiply Handicapped Children.* London: Souvenir Press.

Zatlow, G. (1992) 'Just a sister', *Momentum,* (fall), 13–16.

Zimmerman, M. (1988) 'Mother's health/children's health: informal health care and its health risks', paper (revised) presented at the Annual Meeting of the Midwest Sociological Society, Minneapolis.

Zimmrman, M. (1992) Personal communication in Younghusband, E., Birchall, D., Davie, R. and Pringle, M. L. K. (eds) (1970) *Living with Handicap.* London: National Children's Bureau.

Index